In the Upper Room

FACING THE TRIAL OF YOUR LIFE

JIMMY FOSTER

ISBN 978-1-64028-614-6 (Paperback)
ISBN 978-1-64028-616-0 (Hard Cover)
ISBN 978-1-64028-615-3 (Digital)

Christian Faith Publishing, Inc.
296 Chestnut Street
Meadville, PA 16335
www.christianfaithpublishing.com

All scripture quotations, except where otherwise indicated, are from the King James Version.

Printed in the United States of America

Contents

To my Dad, Ralph "Jobo" Foster, who
passed away in 2012, and my mom,
Myra McTyre Foster, who is still enjoying life at the age of ninety.

They invested their lives to instill values
within me and raised me according
to the precepts of God's Word.

Acknowledgments

I wish to thank Teresa Hughes and
Kim Justinen for their help
proofreading the first draft of this
manuscript.

I would also like to thank Kathy Rainwater
for her help in transcribing the manuscript.

Thanks to my pastor, Dr. Johnny hunt,
whose thoughts on fruitbearing
stimulated my thinking.

I would also like to thank
my mother, Myra Foster,
for allowing me permission to use
some of her poems and other writings
written over fifty years ago.

Introduction

I was pastoring a small country church, and it was time for our Fall Revival. We had scheduled a tremendous lineup of preachers for the week. A lot of hard work had gone into the meeting, and I was eagerly looking forward to the opening service.

The preacher for the first evening was Dr. Johnny Hunt, pastor of the First Baptist Church of Woodstock. The passage he used was the familiar one where the disciples were rowing through a storm on the Sea of Galilee. At the very start of his sermon, he made this statement: "Everyone in the building tonight is either going through a storm, just left a storm, or is about to enter a storm."

I didn't realize it at the time, but I was about to enter one of the most difficult storms of my life. God used that sermon to prepare my heart for what was approaching. It was in the midst of that storm that the idea for this book was born.

One of the common denominators in all human beings is we experience difficulties. It is a universal plight. We are all faced with problems we must solve or puzzles we must figure out. Every day of our lives is filled with minor irritations that distract us from what we have set our hands to accomplish. This is natural and part of life.

There is a point of time, however, when a set of circumstances or a traumatic event takes place that is so overwhelming it tests our character to the limits. It is a crucial and critical moment, a defining moment, that affects us till the day we die. It is what I call *the trial of our lives*. In the balance hangs our emotional and spiritual well-being.

This fire through which we pass can have one of two effects on us. We can come through it stronger than we were before, with character edified and virtue intact, or we can come out consumed with bitterness. If we allow bitterness to take root in our hearts, it will literally rob us of years of our lives.

Christians are not immune. I mean genuine, born-again believers who've been changed by the grace of God will also face these trials. They *will* come our way.

There is no reason, however, why we should be overcome by these occurrences. It *is* possible to go through the storm with a calm and peaceful spirit. Stephen, in the Book of Acts, *literally* was going through the trial of his life. In fact, he would actually lose his life for the stand he took, yet it is recorded of him in Acts 6:15: **"And all that sat in the council, looking steadfastly on him, saw his face as it had been the face of an angel."** Remember, he is going through the trial of his life, yet a supernatural calm and peace so pervaded him that his very countenance reflected the glow of Heaven.

What I'm talking about goes even further than that. We do not have to merely endure the trial peacefully, but it *is* possible to go through the storm *with joy.* The Apostle Paul commended the church at Thessalonica in First Thessalonians 1:6 by saying they received the word **"in much affliction, with joy of the Holy Ghost."** They were afflicted grievously, yet they were noted for the overabounding joy they exhibited. In fact, Jesus himself said: "I am come that they might have life, and that they might have it more abundantly."

When a child of God looks at these examples in scripture and then examines his own feelings as he is going through his particular trial, he may become very perplexed. Often, his feelings don't match the biblical pattern. He begins to think there is something wrong with himself, which adds to his anguish. He usually begins to seek for an answer. He says, "There has got to be a deep, secret formula to having joy." In his search for something complicated, he overlooks the obvious. The answer is found in simplicity. He needs to be reminded that in Christ, he has all he needs to live the Christian life. Christ is sufficient.

How then can a Christian be ruled by peace and calm when it seems like his world is caving in? How exactly does he "achieve" that state of joy and contentment?

I readily confess I proceed from three assumptions that are not open for debate. First, I state categorically that *the Bible is the inspired, inerrant Word of God.* It is trustworthy. Secondly, I will assert to you that *the Bible is relevant to us today.* It is profitable to build our lives on. Thirdly, I reaffirm that *Jesus is exactly who he said he was*—the sinless Son of God, fully man yet God of very God. If any one of these statements is not true, then nothing in this book works, and we have a miserable existence.

Let's take a brief look at these assumptions. I believe the Bible is the inerrant Word of God. As such, it is completely trustworthy.

The person who denies the reliability of the Bible places himself in a dilemma. We have an omnipotent God. By his very nature as God, he is all-powerful. To deny that would make him less than God, yet we are asked to believe this all-powerful God does not have the ability to preserve his Word and keep it from error. What we end up with is a weakling of a deity who cannot even preserve purity in his written Word. This would present us two questions. If he is unable to preserve his Word, then how can he begin and maintain a work within me? If he does not have the ability to preserve his Word, does he deserve the designation "God?"

If any part of the Bible is untrustworthy, then we must toss all of it out. If it cannot be depended upon in the areas of science and history, can we, with confidence, depend upon it in matters of theology or everyday life? I honestly believe the so-called "errors" of the Bible stem from our misunderstanding or our prejudices, not from the Word itself.

I want to assert to you, unequivocally, that the promises of God's Word are *truth.* I can make the above statement about the Word of God as a statement of faith, but I can also make it because it *does* work. That is my deep conviction about the Word of God. I make no apology for that.

Jesus said in John 6:63: **"The words that I speak unto you, they are spirit, and they are life."** His Word is God-breathed. The words he spoke ministered life. Do you want your existence infused with the abundance of life? You will find it in God's Word. How can we develop strength of character? We do it by allowing the Word to shape and conform us into his image. *Where do we get the strength to stand in the day of testing?* We find it as we personally grow and build our lives on the Word of God.

Next, I assert that the Bible is relevant to us today. Any theology or doctrine that has no *practical* value is empty and useless. I believe all the doctrines of the Bible have a practical purpose and are relevant to the struggles we have today. I have attempted to show in this book that the disciples were little different from us today. We have the same difficulties they had, though wrapped in a different time with different technology. In matters concerning the human heart, we can identify with them perfectly. This is one reason why this book will go back and forth from Jesus in the Upper Room to examples in our century. What he said *then* does have meaning for us *now*.

Thirdly, I believe Jesus to be deity, the very essence of God incarnate in the flesh. Jesus made claims about himself. If they were not true, he was a deceiver and is not worthy to be followed. If his claims are not true, he has no ability to grant unto us eternal life. If he is not who he said he was, we can't sing "What a Friend We Have in Jesus." There is no one to reach through the veil of our suffering to give us comfort and strength. There is no one to help us through our trials. But praise God, his character is true, and we can know him personally.

We can see that the strength we find in his words is dependent on these three assumptions. They are the bedrock upon which we can build our lives.

This book is an examination of the words Jesus spoke to his disciples in the Upper Room as portrayed in John chapters 13–17. I have no "deep secret," but I do have an insight on the scripture. It is my desire to point you to that One who can help you through the trials you face.

Some of the illustrations I use in this book come from ministering to other people. Some are composites of a certain type of behavior. Most of the illustrations, I came to realize, are derived from my own personal experiences. They are byproducts of my own personal growth in the Lord. At one point during the writing of this book, I stopped to question whether I should make so many personal references. To do so calls for one to be extremely transparent, and this can be personally uncomfortable. Plus, I questioned whether or not they would be a distraction from the main purpose of the book. I wondered if they might appear self-serving. After weighing the pros and cons of it all, I came to the conclusion that they would not distract but would, rather, validate the main premise of the book. What can illustrate these truths better than an imperfect life that has fought these battles, trusted the Lord, and found his Word to be dependable?

My prayer is God will bless this book and use it to get our eyes off our problems and onto Jesus. May we, together, find strength and comfort in his Word to us. If we can attain that state of joy in the middle of tribulation, then we will be on course as we grow in our relationship with the Lord.

This is a trip through the storm, but it is a trip we don't have to take alone. In the Upper Room, Jesus and the disciples are about to face the darkest storm ever to arise on their horizon. The words he spoke there still speak peace to our hearts as we sail through the storms of our lives.

Chapter 1

LAST WORDS

It was hard to see her this way. The effects of the cancer that had ravaged her body would have been evident to anyone who walked into the room.

Flossie, my grandmother, had always been the perfect picture of joy—a person full of life. When she was amused by something, her deep chuckle—ending with a loud "woo-ee!"— would make any occurrence seem that much funnier to those around her. Her country mannerisms would tickle us teenage boys to death and provided my brother and I with endless material for numerous long-running jokes, like the absurd little notion of what it would be like if Flossie coached our football team. ("Coach Flossie, can I have a Coke?" "Yes, but if you have one now, you can't have one later.") Everything about her said "I love life."

She was the perfect grandmother, illustrating why they placed the word "grand" in grandmother. She was grand in everything she did, especially her cooking. She fried the best chicken I ever ate. Every Saturday, our family would go to Flossie and Granddaddy's house for dinner. At some point, she would inevitably say, "I'm expecting you to eat a big dinner." You just about couldn't walk into the house without her telling you to cut off a piece of cake she had just baked.

It was as if she felt like one of her purposes in life was to fatten up us skinny little kids.

She even looked like a grandmother—close cut gray hair brushed straight back, glasses, hearing aid, and slightly overweight. When I was very young, I thought it was the neatest thing that she was able to take her teeth out and soak them in a glass of water overnight, and in my childlike way of reasoning, I could hardly wait till I got old enough to be able to do the same thing.

Flossie had a deep spiritual side also. Granddaddy was an old time gospel preacher. Flossie could pray and touch Heaven. When Flossie prayed, the hairs on the back of your neck would stand up. I remember the story a preacher told of how one day he had dropped by their house for a visit. Before he could knock on the door, he heard Flossie and Granddaddy praying in the living room together. He was so overwhelmed by the Spirit that swept over him out on the porch that he didn't dare interrupt that holy moment.

Flossie had a deep love and concern for people. While Granddaddy would preach the Word, it was Flossie who would go to the altar to pray with those who came forward. Later at her funeral, it was amazing how many people came by and said, "When I got saved, Flossie was the one who dealt with me."

But now, looking at her in the hospital room, it was difficult to picture her as that same life-loving person. For two years she had suffered from the disease. She had lost a considerable amount of weight and no longer resembled the robust person she had always been. At times, the pain was so great that she would just close her eyes and say "Oh . . . Oh."

In those last times, I do not really remember much what we talked about. I do remember she tried to be the same grandmother and began asking me how I was doing, but soon, the pain would get to her and we would lapse into moments of silence. As I finally got up to leave and was saying goodbye, she gave me a very plaintive look and spoke these words: "I want to go home." They turned out to be the last words I would hear her speak. Instinctively, I knew she was not referring to going home to Joyner Avenue. She was speaking of going home to Jesus. She had been saved as a little girl and had served the Lord faithfully since. As much as she loved life, this world was still not her home.

Some days later, I received a call in the middle of the night from my Mom saying, "I think Flossie is about to go." I threw on some clothes. I confess that I broke some speed limits trying to get there, but by the time I arrived, she had already passed away.

Unless someone has been there, they cannot understand how one feels at that moment immediately after a loved one dies. You can look at the body and know she just is not there. You do not have to check. Something, that spark of life that made her Flossie, was just missing. As I stood there looking at that frail, empty body, her last words came back to me: "I want to go home."

During that painful moment, her last words became a comfort to me. The desire of her heart had been fulfilled. She was at home in the presence of Jesus. There would be no more long nights of suffering through the pain of cancer. There was no sting of death for Flossie. She was with Jesus.

It was Granddaddy's request that after the funeral at the graveside, my brother and I, both ordained ministers, would read the scripture and pray the last prayer before she was laid to rest. It was a difficult thing to do, but as we stood by the graveside with friends and family all around, her last words once again brought comfort and gave strength.

She was home.

* * * * *

The last words of a dying man have always carried great weight in the human experience. In fact, it seems to have a singular importance in our minds. I once played baseball with a young man who threw left-handed. One day, while we were talking baseball, he made the statement, "Actually, I'm a natural right-hander."

Being somewhat puzzled, I asked him, "What in the world are you doing throwing left-handed? Wouldn't it be easier and more natural for you to throw right-handed?"

He answered me, "It was the dying wish of my father for me to be a left-hander."

Chances are, it was not the dying wish of his father. More than likely, it was an offhand comment he made near the time of his death. However, the fact that this young ball player viewed it as his father's last request caused him to radically change the way he played ball, and he spent his playing days doing something that seemed unnatural. To the loved ones who are left, those last words hold great value, and in fact, if they can find no words to cling to, they will search their mind to try and find some.

Not only do those left behind seek for value in last words but also for the one dying, there is the desire to leave something for their family and children. In reading historical accounts of the American Civil War, I have come across descriptions of what the soldiers in the field considered a "good" death. It was not the sudden "you're gone, no pain" death. It was a gradual death, surrounded by his comrades in arms. He could say goodbye to his friends and leave a message for his wife and children. "Give this picture to my wife. Tell her I love her. Tell my children I love them." There was that desire to leave them something to remember him by or leave words of advice or instruction to be an encouragement or comfort through difficult times.

There must have been something of that sense in the life of our Lord Jesus Christ. Years later, as the disciples looked back on the night in the Upper Room, the words Jesus spoke must have been precious words to their hearts for they were truly his last words to them.

Let me set the scene, if I may, as it is portrayed in the Gospel of John, chapters 13–17. It is the time of the Passover. We follow the disciples of Jesus into a spacious upper room that has been prepared for the occasion. As they begin to recline around the spread table, we cannot help but observe a little jockeying for position among the men to see who will sit closest to Jesus. As the supper proceeds, we begin to notice anxiety and confusion on the part of the disciples. So much has transpired in the past week, and each man is lost in his own thoughts, wrapped up in his own little world. Yet in spite of the turmoil of the week, as always, the center of attention, the focus, seems to fall on Jesus.

Jesus, gazing upon these men into whom he has invested so much, knows two things. First, **he knows he is going to die**. He has foretold time after time that he was going to Jerusalem, and he would die. He had even told his disciples that this was the very reason for his coming into the world. He also is aware that the moment is approaching rapidly.

The second thing Jesus knows is **the disciples are about to face the trial of their lives**. They are about to be tested as no one else has ever been tested before. The sheer magnitude of that test is mind-boggling when we think about it. Let's take a look at what they are about to face.

The disciples are about to face *the trial of loss*. They genuinely love Jesus, and they are about to lose him to death. They do not realize yet that it will be just a brief separation. They have not grasped the resurrection. How will they handle the loss of a loved one?

They face *the trial of rejection*. The crowds that cried out "Hosanna! Hosanna to the son of David!" will soon be crying out "Crucify him! Crucify him!" They will see the message they helped take to Israel rejected, and as they flee for their lives, they will feel rejected of man and of God.

Their *faith* will be tested. They have joined with Peter in saying to Jesus "Thou art the Christ, the Son of the Living God" but will find themselves echoing the Emmaus disciples: "We thought it was He who should redeem Israel." Their faith will be shaken to its core. Along with their faith, their *public profession* of that faith will be challenged, and Peter will even say "I know not the man."

Lastly, their *moral courage* will be put on trial. With their lips, they have said, "I would even die for you, Jesus." When it would come down to cases, however, they would show cowardice instead of courage and seek to save themselves.

As Jesus slowly gazes around the room, meeting eye to eye with each of these frail, fragile men, his heart goes out to them. As a dying man, Jesus's desire is to leave something for his own people, something to be a help or strength to them as they face the terrible times ahead. He begins to speak to them his Word—a word that if received would give them a strength of character to be able to stand the storms about to be unleashed upon them.

Too often, a person reads a passage of scripture like this and says "So what? What does that have to do with me?" The truth is human nature is the same today as it was two thousand years ago, and the same trials those men faced back then we still face today.

Let me illustrate this if I can.

THE TRIAL OF LOSS

A young woman receives word that her husband, who is out of state on a business trip, has had a heart attack. The news is that he is in the hospital but appears to be stabilizing. She rushes to see him, but something happens and he dies before she can get there. In her anguish, she cries out, "Why would God take him away from me before I had a chance to say goodbye?" She is facing the trial of loss. How will she respond to it?

Facing loss need not be restricted to the loss of a loved one in death. It may take the form of the loss of financial security or the loss of a dream. A man has worked hard all of his life laboring toward a goal. He has invested his very soul along with time and money to attain security for himself and his family. Suddenly, without warning, he loses his job, and not only does he feel like all that time he spent was wasted but he also stands on the verge of losing all he has already acquired—his home, his car, and sometimes even his family.

Another shape loss may take is the loss of strength. Someone in the ministry may reach the point of burnout. The weight of his responsibilities may so overwhelm him that he feels he is just too weary to go on. He says "I need some time off," and what inevitably happens is he is effectively out of the ministry, usually for good.

Loss is common to all of us, and how we handle it is one of the toughest tests we will ever face.

THE TRIAL OF REJECTION

A young man falls head over heels in love with a young lady. Things seems to be going pretty good for a while but then comes that moment of truth when he asks her to marry him and he finds out the one he loves does not feel the same way. He has been rejected.

Perhaps even more traumatic is the couple who has been married for years, and suddenly, the husband leaves his wife for another woman.

Rejection is one of the most personally devastating things that could happen to us. Nothing contributes more to damaging our self-image than rejection. If we allow ourselves to wallow in the mire of self-pity, we find that Mr. Low Self-Esteem has a distant cousin who comes calling, and his name is Depression.

THE TRIAL OF FAITH

I was visiting in the home of a middle-aged man one visitation night. I have always loved church-wide visitation, and this night was one of those pleasant experiences. We were received cordially and were having a nice conversation with the couple. In my mind, I was saying to myself, "These people are going to be receptive to the gospel."

It came to that point in the conversation when I felt that the time was right, and I said to the man, "Let me ask you a question. Have you come to the place in your life where you know that you have eternal life and that you will go to Heaven when you die?"

His pleasant countenance changed. It was not a look of anger, but you could almost see the years of bitter, harsh feelings reflected in his face. He stated he had been saved as a youth and gave a good verbal testimony to it, but then he added, "But I don't go to church anymore."

When I asked him why not, he began to tell me a sadly familiar story about a church split. Somehow, in the midst of it all, he had taken his eyes off Jesus and looked at the people in the church. He became so disillusioned by what he saw that he said, "I'm never going back." His faith had been tried and found lacking.

Christians who remain faithful to the Lord and his church may also find their faith tested. We have been told by the world "the workplace is no place for religion" or "don't speak of God in our schools." When there is a holy prompting to give a witness, peer pressure says "You're not one of *those* are you?" The question is will we boldly be identified with Christ? Will our faith and public profession pass the test?

THE TRIAL OF MORAL COURAGE

All of us have heard preachers thunder from the pulpit: "If you were given the choice to renounce your faith or die, how many of you would have the moral courage to die for the sake of Jesus?"

Many Christians in other parts of the world have been asked to make that choice, but here in America, none of us have been asked to do that—yet. I am of the opinion that if a person will not live for Jesus, then he will not die for him. Maybe the question we should be asking is not who will die for Jesus but *who has the moral courage to live for him?*

In a society where immorality is rampant and accepted, who has the courage to stand and say "There is a standard for right and wrong, and God's Word is the final authority"? When temptation, which can so easily overtake us, tries to ensnare us, who has the intestinal fortitude to say "I may be a weak vessel, but by the grace of God and his enabling power, I will be pure"?

With the challenges we face in the twenty-first century, our biggest challenge may be to live above reproach for his glory.

It would seem then that things have not changed all that much. Our trials may come packaged a little differently, but we basically face the same tests that the disciples did.

If there is value in the words of a dying man, then consider the worth of what the very Son of God spoke to his own. Are we facing a trial? Are we about to enter one? The Words of Jesus are precious. They were given for a specific purpose. They were given to prepare us, encourage us, and strengthen our faith so we might stand strong and steady during the storms that sweep around us.

Jesus would speak other words. He would speak to them, for three days later, he would rise from the grave. He would give them his parting words on the Mount of Olives, but in the Upper Room, he gave them his last words before his death—his concluding council before their trial.

Let us now turn our thoughts back to that band of men gathered in communion around the table. From the Upper Room come echoes of words spoken by the Lamb of God. They are his last words—some final instructions given to guide us through the trial of our lives.

The Scripture

THE SAVIOR'S LOVE

"Now before the feast of the Passover, when Jesus knew that his hour was come that he should depart out of this world unto the Father, having loved his own which were in the world, he loved them unto the end."

—John 13:1

"He that loveth me shall be loved of the Father, and I will love him, and will manifest myself to him."

—John 14:21

"This is my commandment, that you love one another, as I have loved you. Greater love hath no man than this that a man lay down his life for his friends."

—John 15:12-13

Chapter 2

THE SAVIOR'S LOVE

It was just a silly little child's game. It had not popped into his mind in over twenty years, and he did not understand why its memory should suddenly dog his steps now.

He was in the fifth grade. It was during the 60s—about the time the Beatles were becoming popular and were first touring the United States. All of the kids in his class were swept up in Beatlemania.

Of course, all the guys in the class had short hair; many of them flat tops. Naturally, the parents were extremely reluctant to allow their child to let their hair grow out like one of the Beatles. In fact, initially, most would flatly refuse. However, there was an ingenious way to get around all that, which would allow kids to be instantly transformed into a Beatle. You could buy a Beatle wig, and any time you desired, you could have the longer hair and characteristic bangs of a Beatle.

It happened at recess one day. One of the boys had brought his Beatle wig to school, and everyone was playing this little game. One of the boys would put on the Beatle wig, and all the girls would emit the telltale scream of adolescent idol worship, shout "it's a Beatle," and begin to chase him all over the yard. When the boy got tired or found himself boxed in a corner, he would take off the wig and toss it to one of the other guys. He would put it on, and the girls would scream "it's a Beatle" again and the chase would resume.

It really looked like a lot of fun to him. He said to himself, "I've got to get in on this." So he laid his ball glove down and tried to get closer to the action. Soon his opportunity came. The current Beatle, after running around in circles for a while, snatched the wig off his head and tossed it to him. Expectantly, he grabbed the wig, put it on, and turned to run.

No one screamed.

No one chased him.

All the girls stood there with a disgusted look that said "Why don't you take that thing off your head?" He took it off and tossed it to the next guy. There was the scream, and the game began again.

He felt foolish. But kids have a tendency to recover from those things rather quickly, and soon, he had his glove on and was playing ball. He forgot all about the incident, and it did not enter his mind again.

But now it is twenty-five years later. He had just been rejected by someone he cared for. For years, he has been struggling with a very low image of himself. He is reluctant to try anything the least bit risky, much less follow one of his dreams for fear of failure. At times, he feels that he just does not have the abilities others have. He has a reserved nature and does not socialize easily. He has tried very hard to overcome these feelings of inadequacy and has made some progress. But now, after enduring the heartbreak of rejection, a long-forgotten memory of a child's game pops back into his head. Now he does not feel like the mature adult that he is. The confidence he has tried to develop forsakes him. In his mind's eye, he is no longer thirty years old. He is that little boy out on the playground, and this is the way he feels about himself.

I'm not worth anything.

I'm not as good as other people.

There is no way anyone could love someone like me.

* * * * *

Feelings of inadequacy plague a vast number of people, and it seems like the longer I serve in ministry that I encounter it more and more. Low self-esteem will cause a person to be less than they could be and fail to accomplish their goals in life.

Do not make the mistake of confusing low self-esteem with humility. Humility is a godly virtue. Low self-esteem is destructive. Allow me to explain the difference.

In the Christian's life, humility recognizes our submission to Christ and, therefore, does not seek to promote self. Humility is an honest, correct view of self. Humility *does allow* for the recognition of strong points, but it does not trumpet them or brag about abilities. It tempers cockiness with recognition of a person's nature. I am a human being with faults and failures. I have a sin nature to contend with. I know, however, that God saw something of worth in me.

Low self-esteem, on the other hand, sees no strong points. It is personally destructive. A person who struggles with it will find their creativity affected. Why attempt anything when nothing I do will have any value?

Low self-esteem can lead to depression, and depression incapacitates. The person swallowed up by depression does not have the motivation to do anything. In fact, this is the way satanic oppression operates in an individual's life. A doubt is planted in a man's mind. As he begins to struggle with that doubt, depression sets in, tormenting his mind. The depression incapacitates him, and if unchecked, it effectively ends his service for the Lord, which is our adversary's aim for our lives.

We can see, therefore, that low self-esteem must be dealt with for us to enjoy a full, productive life for the Lord. How then can we combat this destructive tendency?

Only one thing can counter low self-esteem, and that is to know there is someone who totally, consistently loves us. Humans have a built-in need to have someone give them unqualified love. Unfortunately, we live in a society that makes no commitment with the words "I love you." People can, without remorse, leave someone they have said they love. However, I can depend upon *one constant love*. I can with confidence rest in the assurance that Jesus loves me.

Two things assure me that he loves me. First, if he thought enough of me to die for me, then I am *of value to the Savior*. Make no mistake, we are not worthy of his love, but we are *worth something* to Jesus. Nothing in me caused Jesus to love me, but something in Jesus causes him to love me. And because he loves me, he considers me one of his prized possessions—something of value.

The second thing that assures me of his love is the fact that he spends time talking with me every day. Even this morning, I had a wonderful time of fellowship with him as he spoke to me out of his Word. Just think, the Creator, the Almighty God who holds the universe in his hand, thinks enough of me to speak to me. That is awesome! I must be somebody.

Because I know this, I have come to a realization that absolutely nothing can shake. I will never be unloved. No matter what the world throws at me, which friend may fail or forsake me, *there is always someone who loves me*. His name is Jesus. Not only that, but his love can also boost my self-image. I do not need to think of myself as inferior. I was made in the image of God, and I am an object of his love.

The love of Jesus has a healing quality. A person who has been hurt either emotionally or spiritually can experience a healing balm as his love wraps around us. Nothing can soothe the pain like a good healthy dose of his love.

Such a beautiful picture of Jesus's love radiates from the Upper Room. The first thing Jesus said to his disciples was not spoken by words. They were spoken by actions. I have always been one to believe actions over words. Words can be thrown about rather easily. Proving what we say by our actions is much more difficult.

Jesus's entire life had been one long "I love you." When Jesus spoke of love, the disciples could believe it for they had seen it demonstrated in his life. In fact, the first thing we see in the Upper Room is an action as Jesus washed the disciples' feet. In a few short hours, Jesus would show his love in the ultimate way. **"But God demonstrates his own love towards us, in that while we were still sinners, Christ died for us"** (Rom. 5:8, NKJV).

As we look at John 13:1, we notice several things about his love.

JESUS'S CLAIM TO OWNERSHIP

The first thing we notice is Jesus's claim to ownership. (**"Having loved his own which were in the world."**) The love of Jesus is a personal love. Jesus looked upon his disciples and said, "They are mine. They belong to me." In fact, the Lord is possessive of his children. Since the Lord is that particular about his children, he takes it personally when someone lashes out at one of his.

We can see this illustrated in scripture. When Saul of Tarsus, who had persecuted the church, met Jesus on the road to Damascus, Jesus did not say to him, "Saul, why are you persecuting my church?" His words were "Why do you persecute *me*?" His love was such that he considered any attack on his children an attack on himself. He took it personally.

When the disciples tried to prevent some from bringing children unto the Lord, the scripture says Jesus was displeased and rebuked the disciples. He took up for the little children.

Are you one of his? Rest assured. He loves you with a very personal love. Are you facing a trial? He will take your case.

As one who rightfully claims ownership of us by virtue of his shed blood, Christ has a longing for fellowship with us. Luke 22:15 records Jesus speaking in the Upper Room: **"With desire I have desired to eat this Passover with you before I suffer."** The Greek word translated as *desire*, *epithumia*, indicates "a longing for." The English word *desire* does not really convey the strength behind the original. Its root indicates "a passion toward" and in some places in scripture is translated *lust*.

Do you see the emotions displayed here? It indicates an object so desired that it is rushed at and seized with a passion. That is how strong his desire is to fellowship with us. When we take time to fellowship with him, he delights in those moments. It really is a personal, possessive love he has for us.

IT IS NOT A BLIND LOVE

We have all heard the saying "Love is blind." What that saying means is when somebody is in love, they become blind to the person's faults.

It is not that they just overlook those faults. They absolutely cannot see them. The amazing thing about his love is it is not blind. It is love "with your eyes open."

Jesus, **knowing his hour**, loved his disciples. As omnipotent deity, Jesus not only "knew his hour" but also "knew his disciples." He knew their personality quirks. He knew Thomas's tendency to doubt. He knew Peter's propensity toward shooting off his big mouth. He knew of James and John's ambition. He knew them intimately because he had made them, yet *he still loved them.*

Have you ever felt that your flaws make you inadequate? He knows you intimately and still loves you. He has even numbered the hairs of your head (and he knows how quickly they are falling out). He loves us, warts and all.

This is all the more amazing, for he knows everything about us. He is the one who made us. He does not see the façade—the me I try to show to all those around. He knows what I am actually thinking. He knows the thoughts that are not exactly pure and holy, yet he loves me still.

THE EXTENT OF HIS LOVE

Human love has its limits. We have a tendency to love only as far as we are loved. As long as someone treats us right, we will reciprocate that love. It is easy to love that way. It is easy to love the lovely. But just let someone cross us, and it is not so easy. Oh, we may even forgive them more than once, but there is a limit to how much we will take. We will be hurt just so many times till we say "That's it! I've had it! I won't take it anymore!"

The question could be asked then: just how far would *his* love go? Jesus, **having loved his own which were in the world, loved them unto the end**.

I want you to notice what it does not say. It does not say he loved them till they denied him. It does not say he loved them till they turned tail and ran. It does not say he loved them till he grew weary of them. It also does not say he loved them until he decided to love someone else. He loved them *unto the end*. In fact, it really went further than that, for his death was not the end. Three days later, that love was burning even more fervently. Nothing can stop his love.

First Corinthians 13:4–8 describes love in general and describes his love perfectly: **"Love suffers long and is kind; love does not envy; love does not parade itself, is not puffed up; does not behave rudely, does not seek its own, is not provoked, thinks no evil; does not rejoice in iniquity, but rejoices in the truth; bears all things, believes all things, hopes all things, endures all things.** Love never fails" (NKJV).

Someone may ask, "If his love never fails, what happens if I sin? Will he cease to love me?" No, nothing can shake his love. It is still there, but sin will break my fellowship with him. Because of his holiness, he must respond to that sin. He will do this through the convicting presence of the Holy Spirit calling you to repentance. If you do not yield to his urging, then the Bible teaches that he chastens his children. Bear in mind, however, that his warnings and corrections concerning sin are a reflection of his love, for he only wants you to experience his best for your life. In the mist of all of this, his love stands steady and unfailing.

How far would his love go? It went all the way to Calvary's cross. How strong is it? It is stronger than death. How far is its reach? It reaches all the way down into the gutter and lifts up the down and out. It cleans him up, changes him, and makes him a child of God.

With a love that far-reaching, who could speak of love with more authority than Jesus?

HIS COMMANDMENT OF LOVE

Because Jesus had already shown his love to the disciples, he could then instruct them about love. He first gives them a command to love and then gives a brief synopsis of the type of love he was talking about.

"This is my commandment, that you love one another" (John 15:12). It is impossible for a Christian to be obedient and not love. This is not a suggestion. It is not even just a good thing to do. We are commanded to love one another. To fail to love is to be willfully disobedient to the command of our Lord. That is why it is impossible to love God and hate your brother.

I can just hear someone saying, "Some people you just can't love." I'm not saying it is always easy to love some folks, but it *is* possible to love them. Jesus would not command you to do something that was impossible to do. Sometimes it takes his grace, but you can do it.

What you must understand is love is a choice. We have developed this idea that love is something mysterious that just happens to us; something ethereal that is beyond our control. The truth is we choose whom we will love. That is why if a couple *really wants* a marriage to work, it will, because the couple chooses to love each other and puts the necessary effort into it.

Similarly, as a Christian, I can determine that I am going to love. When Christ loves through me like that, I can love people in spite of their failings.

After giving the commandment, Jesus then tells the disciples how to love. He said to love **"as I have loved you."** The pattern they were to follow was Jesus. They were to love as Jesus loved. That meant the giving of themselves totally for the good of others. To love like Jesus would abolish selfishness for we would always consider others above ourselves.

Jesus's description of love follows in verse 13: **"Greater love hath no man than this, than a many lay down his life for his friends."** He would graphically demonstrate that love the next day on a Roman cross. The greatest possible example of love would be to die for a friend. Jesus went further than that because he died for me before I even knew him.

How many of us are willing to give of our time, our money, and ourselves to carry the gospel to others or to meet their physical needs? How many of us truly love the way Jesus loved?

As portrayed in the Upper Room, we see his love as personal, never ending, and given with the full knowledge of our shortcomings. Since we have one who loves us so, we have no reason to feel unloved, and with *his* love, we can turn and love those around us. *That* is the most fulfilling, satisfying life a human soul can live.

For the person who might be tempted to say "that sounds too simplistic," let me make a confession. The story I told at the beginning of this chapter is a true account. I can attest to its veracity because I was that little boy on the playground. For a great deal of my life, I struggled with a feeling of inferiority. I know what that feeling is like.

I can also attest to the fact that it can be overcome. In fact, I have some friends who would say I have swung too far in the other direction. They would say that not only do I have unbounded confidence in my abilities but also have too high an opinion of myself. Now it seems that the problem I deal with is an ego.

Can the idea expressed in a simple child's song, "Yes, Jesus Loves Me," really make that big a difference in a person's life? The answer is *yes*.

Let me be very transparent about all this. *His love was always there*, and I came to know him at a very early age. So through much of my struggle, I was a Christian. I believed in the idea that Jesus loves me, yet I still had a problem with it. It was only as I grew in the grace of our Lord that I began to fully appreciate his love. As I began to spend time with Jesus in fellowship and in his Word, I began to comprehend and become more aware of the love that had been there all along. You must understand that the Christian life is a continual process of growth. It is a lifelong process. I am still growing. I hope I am still growing and learning on the day I die.

This realization and the change it brings is a genuine modern-day miracle. If your test has caused you to doubt your worth or if it has been a result of your self-image, listen very carefully. You do not have to be miserable. You can rejoice that Jesus loves you, and if you will just take notice, he will express it to you in a thousand different ways every day.

> **"He that loveth me shall be loved of the Father, and I will love him, and will manifest myself to him."**
>
> —John 14:21

The Scripture

THE SERVANT'S HEART

"But Jesus called them unto him and said, Ye know that the princes of the Gentiles exercise dominion over them, and they that are great exercise authority upon them. But it shall not be so among you; but whosoever will be chief among you, let him be your servant: Even as the Son of man came not to be ministered unto, but to minister, and to give his life a ransom for many."

—Matthew 20:25–28

"Jesus knowing that the Father had given all things into his hands, and that he was come from God, and that he went to God; he riseth from supper, and laid aside his garments; and took a towel, and girded himself. After that he poureth water into a basin, and began to wash the disciples' feet, and to wipe them with the towel wherewith he was girded.

Then cometh he to Simon Peter: and Peter saith unto him, Lord, dost thou wash my feet?

Jesus answered and said unto him, What I do thou knowest not now; but thou shalt know hereafter.

Peter said unto him, Thou shalt never wash my feet.

Jesus answered him, If I wash thee not, thou hast no part with me.

Simon Peter saith unto him, Lord not my feet only, but also my hands and my head.

Jesus saith unto him, he that is washed needeth not save to wash his feet, but is clean every whit: and ye are clean, but not all. For he knew who should betray him; therefore said he, Ye are not all clean.

So after he had washed their feet, and had taken his garments, and was set down again, he said unto them, Know ye what I have done to you? Ye call me Master and Lord: and ye say well; for so I am. If I then, your Lord and Master, have washed your feet: ye also ought to wash one another's feet. For I have given you an example, that you should do as I have done to you. Verily, verily, I say unto you, The servant is not greater than his lord; neither he that is sent greater than he that sent him.

If ye know these things, happy are ye if ye do them."

—John 13:3–17

Chapter 3

THE SERVANT'S HEART

Peter could still remember the conversation vividly. The audacity of James and John had nearly left him speechless, but true to form, he had recovered and had his say. He had tried to be big about it, but there is just so much a person could take.

It had all started a few days earlier when James and John's mother, Salome, had indicated that she had a request of Jesus. Peter wondered what it was all about. There she was kneeling before Jesus with her two boys standing a few steps back. As she began to speak, he stood there in disbelief at what he was hearing.

"Master, if you consider me a virtuous and honorable woman, please grant me a request."

Jesus, looking her straight in the eye, had asked, "What is it that you want?"

"Lord, see my two boys here? They are such fine, deserving boys. When you set up your kingdom, would you grant them to sit one on your right hand and one on your left hand?"

Peter nearly gagged out loud. "I'll bet you James and John put her up to this," he thought. "Where do they get off thinking they deserve that spot? Do they really think they have what it takes? When there were many who left the Master, wasn't it I who said, 'To whom could we turn? You have the words of eternal life. You are the Christ, the Son of the Living God.' Who else around here has that kind of faith and backbone?"

Peter noticed all the other disciples. He could see the indignation rising in them and thought, "Yeah, they know."

Jesus, his voice steady, said, "You really don't understand what it is you are asking." Turning his attention to James and John, he addressed them with a question. "Are you able to drink the cup I drink of, or to be baptized with the baptism I am about to be baptized in?"

James and John expectantly stepped forward, nearly stumbling in their anxiousness. Peter found it almost comical the way they blurted out in unison "Yes, we are."

Jesus gave a slight sigh and said in a near whisper, "You *will* drink the cup that I drink of, and it will be a bitter cup, but to grant that type of honor is not mine to give. That is reserved for my Father to grant."

Jesus then began to teach them about being great, ending with the assertion, "If you want to be great in God's eyes, be the servant of all." Peter barely heard him. The resentment swelling within him closed his ears.

Jesus rose to continue his journey toward Jerusalem. The disciples began to gather their effects together and proceeded to follow Jesus in the way.

Once they were on the road, Peter sought out James and John. "Just who do you think you are?" he fairly hissed under his breath. "What makes you think you're so great? You never saw the things I was able to do when Jesus sent us out by twos. I was even able to cast out demons. I have as much claim to those positions as you do."

Before long, all the disciples were embroiled in the controversy; all were speaking in hushed tones lest Jesus overhear them.

Suddenly, Jesus stopped and turned toward his disciples. Knowingly Jesus asked, "What are you discussing?"

An awkward silence settled over them. Everyone was just a little embarrassed to admit what they been talking about. "This is just great!" thought Peter. "He always seems to know what is going on."

Without waiting for an answer, Jesus gestured toward a small child being held by his mother as they traveled down the road. "Whoever receives this child in my name receives me, and whoever receives me receives the Father. For he who is *least* among you *will be great.*"

Yes, Peter remembered every word of the dispute. Now here they were celebrating the Passover, and it still ate on his insides. He could not seem to get over it all, and he wondered if he would ever view his friends in quite the same way. He felt like there was a slight frigidity in their relations that had not been there before. He had even noticed a certain vying for position to see who would sit nearest to Jesus. Why, John, as small as he was, had virtually squeezed between two of them to sit next to Jesus.

Peter could hardly believe what his eyes were seeing now. Jesus got up from the table, laid aside his outer garment, took a towel, and began pouring water into a basin. "What is he about to do now," mused Peter.

Slowly, Jesus, beginning with Matthew, took the basin and began to wash the disciples' feet. Peter was thunderstruck. This was the action of a slave! What was the Master doing washing *our* feet.

One by one, the countenances of the disciples changed as the Lord took each of their feet. The haughty look of pride was transformed to one of shame as they realized just how petty their argument was. There's just something about genuine humility that puts a spotlight on a sham.

Peter thought to himself, "This isn't right for the Lord to wash our feet. Why aren't the others saying anything? I know what I would say."

Then Jesus came to Peter and gently took one of his feet.

"This isn't right. No, no, never. You will never wash *my* feet!"

* * * * *

I have used a little bit of imagination in my recreating of the events. We do not really know what Peter or the other disciples were thinking, but it is evident in scripture that there was a huge controversy that threatened to disrupt the unity of the band of disciples. The responsible culprit was named *ambition*.

It is sad to have to admit, but there are often problems that arise in churches that can disrupt the fellowship and cause divisions. More often than not, it proves to be a power struggle, fueled by ambition. Who is going to control the church? I *am* going to have my say. It's going to be *my way* or *no way*. We've been here for years, this was my granddaddy's church, and we've never done it that way.

An insidious first cousin to ambition goes by the name *pride*. Peter's response "You will never wash my feet," though intended to sound pious, was born, I believe, of pride. When a person's pride is stung, reason is thrown to the winds. Everything that happens is viewed as a personal affront, and you try to see hidden motives where there are none.

Ambition and pride can also cause disruptions both in the business world and at home. Not only is it destructive but also deceptive. When the confusion that naturally accompanies this kind of behavior occurs, often the person responsible never realizes that it is an outgrowth of his own actions, and he has to find someone or something to blame it on. It's a difficult truth to accept that many of the trials we face are brought about by our own actions.

If we may, let's try to draw a thumbnail sketch or paint a picture of the man driven by blind ambition.

The overly ambitious man is usually a man of talent and abilities, but he is one who is very self-serving. The world revolves around him. He has a strong will and always has to express his viewpoint. At the same time, he will never give any credence to another person's viewpoint. He will sometimes have a problem with authority. There is always conflict surrounding him.

This man will do anything to get ahead. Ethics are optional. He will bend any moral code if it will attain his goal. He will then call it only a minor infraction. To achieve what he desires, he will walk over anybody, even friends. He is always pointing out the failings of others, mistakenly feeling that it makes himself appear better qualified.

He is a workaholic; therefore, his family life suffers as he gives more time to the job than his family. He tries to justify it by saying

"I'm doing this for you," but by his actions, he is saying, "Relationships are a secondary distraction and a necessary evil."

His is a life of stress.

Jesus saw the seed of this pernicious trait planted within his disciples, and lest it grow and consume them Jesus attacked the problem head on.

JESUS'S TEACHING CONCERNING THE SERVANT'S HEART

The main thrust of Jesus's teaching was that *the way to be great was to be a servant.*

He presented this concept by contrasting it with the Gentile rules. These rulers would lord over their subjects or literally flaunt their power. An example of this was Pilate sitting in judgment over the Son of God. His statement was, "Do you not know I have the power of life and death over you?" There is a certain arrogance involved in wielding power in this fashion. Though the consequences may not be so dire, we see the same arrogance displayed in the way the world manipulates its authority. There is the supervisor at work who says "Don't you know I have the power to fire you?" There is the government official who says "I will break you." There is the attorney who says "We will take you to court and sue you for your last dime." It seems like the spirit of Pilate is alive and well in this age.

In God's economy, things are different. Greatness in the eyes of God consists in being a servant. The person who gives himself unselfishly is truly a great man.

Next, he emphasized *the way to calm the chaos brought about by pride and ambition was to be in submission to others.* There was a very real danger that the discord among the disciples would permanently damage their unity and love for one another. They were showing the same characteristics as a modern-day church split.

God places a special premium on unity. **"Behold, how good and pleasant it is for brethren to dwell together in unity!"** (Ps. 133:1) As long as it was not over an essential matter, it would be better for his disciples to be in submission to one another and preserve unity.

Finally, he taught that *fulfillment is found in serving others*. This is what Jesus meant when, after washing the disciples' feet, he said, **"If ye know these things,** happy are ye **if ye do them"** (verse 17). In short, Jesus was teaching them that there was no greater satisfaction in life than to serve or help others in need. It is intrinsically self-rewarding.

This was what the Lord was trying to teach the disciples. Unfortunately, like many of us, they were guilty of selective hearing. Basically, they heard what they wanted to hear and chose not to hear what was personally uncomfortable.

THE DEMONSTRATION OF A SERVANT'S HEART

Since Jesus knew his words were not sinking in, he sought to graphically illustrate what he was saying to them. He did this by performing the task of a slave—washing the disciples' feet.

In examining this passage of scripture, I want you to notice first *the Savior's position*. Verse 3 of chapter 13 states that Jesus was fully aware of three things about himself: the Father had given all things into his hand, he came from God, and he was returning to God.

The Book of Colossians is a good companion book to go with a study of his position. Colossians 1:18–20 states: **"And he is the head of the body, the church: who is the beginning, the firstborn from the dead; that in all thing he might have the preeminence. For it pleased the Father that in him should all fullness dwell; And, having made peace through the blood of his cross, by him to reconcile all things unto himself; by him, I say, whether they be things in earth, or things in heaven."**

We can see in this passage that all things are to be in subjections to him. Not only is the church, everything in Heaven, and all that walk the earth to be in subjection to him, but it is also through his blood that all things are to be reconciled to God. As the preeminent one, he is SOVEREIGN, and he is LORD. All things have been given into his hands.

He knew he came from God. Once again, the Book of Colossians goes into great detail to describe our Lord. It calls him **the image of**

the invisible God. It states that he was involved in creation by saying **by him were all things created**. In fact, we were created for his pleasure, for it states **all things were created by him and for him**. His eternal nature and power are asserted when it says that **he is before all things, and by him all things consist**. He came from God for HE WAS GOD.

He knew he was going back to God. This knowledge revealed his confidence in his own resurrection. He had, time after time, predicted his own death, but all along, he could look beyond the grave to a resurrection and ascension where he would take his rightful place. He would return VICTORIOUS over the grave.

It is amazing that in the light of such plain scripture, some who claim to be followers of him would deny his nature. It is evident in scripture that he is sovereign Lord, he is victorious, and he is God. That is his position.

I want you to notice not only his position but also *the Savior's pattern*.

If anyone could boast of his birthright or greatness, it was Jesus, yet he demonstrated his humility by washing the disciples' feet. By showing them with actions, Jesus was trying to reveal to them just how far they were from being a true servant. Their attitudes, not their words, were very revealing in this respect.

Jesus's teaching was more than just with words. His actions and lifestyle reflected what he said. He never sought to promote himself, but he sought to do the Father's will. By this action, he sought to bring out the best in the disciples.

After washing their feet, he told them, "I have done this for an example of how you are to conduct yourselves. If I, your Lord and Master, have stooped to wash your feet you are to follow my example and be a servant to others."

If we are his disciples, students of his way, we are to follow his example. The servant is not greater than his Lord. To be a servant, to display a servant's heart, is to be in submission to the Lordship of Jesus. He set the pattern for us to follow.

The question to be asked is whether he is rightfully LORD? The answer is an undeniable YES. Then for a Christian to be self-serving is to, in practicality, reject his lordship over our lives.

THE CHARACTERISTICS OF A SERVANT'S HEART

If it is that important for us to be servant, to let him shine through us, then what are some of the characteristics that should be evident in our lives? What are the characteristics of a servant's heart?

The first thing I would like for you to consider is *the servant's attitude*. He does not serve grudgingly. In fact, he is not coerced into doing the things he does. First and foremost, he has an attitude of SUBMISSION. He is in submission to his Lord. Whatever his Lord's desire is, that is his desire. In all things, he is in submission. If this is a man's heartbeat, it will even show through on his job. He will not be a malcontent. There will be no spirit of complaining or rebellion. He will be in submission to his supervisor.

He will show a WILLINGNESS to do any job and whatever is necessary to get the task done. Along with that willingness, there will be a CONTENTMENT that permeates his efforts.

The true servant's heart will have NO DESIRE FOR PERSONAL RECOGNITION. He is not doing it for reward or recognition. He sees a need and is only interested in meeting that particular need. I used a phrase earlier: "intrinsically self-rewarding." This is the way a servant's heart views it. Knowing that someone was helped is reward enough.

I once had a deacon get very upset with me. In our church, we had a teenage boy who had helped me do some things to prepare for our upcoming revival. I like to encourage that in young people, and I made a point to thank him publicly from the pulpit. This evidently hit this deacon wrong. He really felt like he had been slighted for not being recognized for all *he* did (which, to be brutally honest, was not that much as he was not faithful to his responsibilities as a deacon).

In one particular gripe session, he made this statement; "I don't do all that I do for any glory of my own. I gladly do it for the church, but you never recognize all we deacons do."

My own response to him was, "If you're not doing it for your own glory, then why are you upset that you didn't get receive any recognition?"

I am not picking on deacons here. Thank God we have many deacons who *do* have a servant's heart, but this man knew nothing about being a servant. His attitude was a self-serving one. He enjoyed the position and recognition, but he was not a servant.

I would like for you to notice next *the servant's consideration.* The servant is always putting OTHER PEOPLE'S NEEDS AHEAD OF HIS OWN. He has a thoughtfulness that is extraordinary.

Unfortunately, I know some preachers who put their ministries before people. They will use people when it is necessary to build their ministry. If they perceive a person to be a threat to their ministry, then they will try to hurt that person. They are so concerned with their ministry that they forget that those people *are* their ministry. They are the reason we are in the ministry in the first place.

The preacher who is a servant says "How can I minister in love to my flock? What are their needs?" He never compromises a principle and sometimes has to deal with problems head on, but he always does it in a spirit of love.

Also along the lines of a servant's consideration is the fact that the servant is A MAN OF AMBITION. This may sound contradictory to what I have said earlier in this chapter, but there is a very real distinction in what I am describing here. The servant is ambitious to accomplish FOR THE LORD. It is not personal ambition, but he is motivated to uplift the name of Jesus. He wants his life to honor and glorify the Lord. He desire for everyone to know how wonderful Jesus is and is consumed by a passion to make his name known. That is his consideration.

Finally, I would like to point out *how the servant works.* He works cheerfully, ENTHUSIASTICALLY, doing all he does as unto the Lord. Whether in the church or on the job, he does it heartily as a testimony for the Lord.

Not only does he work enthusiastically, but he also utilizes all of his talents to the BEST OF HIS ABILITIES. He generally does more than he is called upon to do. He goes above and beyond the call of duty.

Luke 17:7–9 speaks of the servant who only does what is required of him as an "unprofitable servant." The one who does more than is expected is of great profit to his church and to mankind as a whole.

If you are like me, when you really take a look at the servant's heart, you will find that you fall far short of being a profitable servant of God. We may be strong in some areas but weak in others. I am being perfectly honest when I say I am not there yet, but my heart's desire is to have the true heart of a servant.

Until the day I can say there is no pride in my heart, I have no personal ambition in my life, and I do all I can and more for the Lord, then I will need to work on this area of my life.

Is there joy in being a servant to others? Yes, it is a promise of the Lord. Let us, therefore, be obedient to the commands of scripture.

"Servant, obey in all things our masters in the flesh, not with eye-service, as men pleasers, but in sincerity of heart, fearing God.

And whatever you do, do it heartily, as to the Lord and not to men, knowing that from the Lord you will receive the reward of inheritance; for you serve the Lord Christ."

—Colossians 3:22–24 (NKJV)

The Scripture

THE CURE FOR A TROUBLED HEART

PART I

"When Jesus had thus said, he was troubled in spirit, and testified, and said, Verily, verily, I say unto you, that one of you shall betray me.

Little children, yet a little while I am with you. Ye shall seek me: and as I said unto the Jews, Whither I go, ye cannot come; so now I say to you. A new commandment I give unto you, that ye love one another. By this shall all men know that ye are my disciples, if ye have love one to another.

Simon Peter said unto him, Lord, whither goest thou?

Jesus answered him, Whither I go, thou canst not follow me now; but thou shalt follow me afterwards.

Peter said unto him, Lord, why cannot I follow thee now? I will lay down my life for thy sake.

Jesus answered him, Wilt thou lay down thy life for my sake? Verily, verily, I say unto thee. The cock shall not crow, till thou hast denied me thrice. Let not your heart be troubled: ye believe in God, believe also in me. In my Father's house are many mansions: if it were not so, I would have told you. I go to prepare a place for you. And if I go and prepare a place for you, I will come again, and receive you unto myself; that where I am, there ye may be also."

—John 13:21, 33–14:3

Chapter 4

THE CURE FOR A TROUBLED HEART

PART I

THE THINGS THAT TROUBLE OUR HEARTS

My dad loves to tell a story about my brother and me that I love to hear. It happened when I was so young that I barely remember it.

My brother Johnny is two years older than me; therefore, throughout most of our childhood, he was much bigger than I was. This kind of gave Johnny a self-confident attitude that he could outdo me in most any game we would play. In fact, he actually could in many things, much as I hate to admit it. As will happen with all children, he had gotten a little cocky about it.

He had the ability (which, by the way, he has outgrown) to get one up on me or to play me for a sucker. I can still remember when I was about to go out for midget football for the first time, Johnny said he was going to "help" me. He then proceeded to run me through some drills he had contrived called "work-overs." It basically consisted of him being able to beat up on me, saying it was designed to toughen me up. Like an idiot, I allowed him to do this, thinking he was doing me some big favor. Aren't older brothers wonderful? Aren't little brothers gullible?

There was one day, though, when the tables were turned.

Dad, Johnny, and I were out in the front yard playing. Johnny and Dad were throwing the football around. I was off to the side playing with some toys, seeming unaware of what they were doing.

Johnny would run a pass pattern, and Dad would pass it to him. After he caught the ball, he would turn downfield and start doing these fancy little dance steps, avoiding imaginary tacklers, and ended up scoring touchdown after touchdown. He would then trot back to Dad, listening to the fanciful cheering of an imaginary crowd. They continued playing, running patterns, and catching passes, never thinking I was paying any attention to them at all.

Finally, my opportunity came. Johnny ran a pattern in my direction. I set my toys down and got ready. Johnny caught the ball and was just starting to turn up field, expecting the same nonexistent tacklers he could sidestep. At that precise moment—POW!—I nailed him. He went down hard with a stunned look of surprise on his face.

I calmly got up without a word, turned around, walked back to my toys, and resumed my playing.

The shocked look on Johnny's face quickly turned to anger. He stormed over to where I was and began hollering, "You only did that because you caught me by surprise. You could never really tackle me. Get up, and I'll prove it to you. Get up, and let's play for real! Dad, make Jimmy get up and play for real!"

I ignored him and kept on playing with my toys. I didn't have anything to prove. I'd already taken him down.

Here is the scene then: I'm sitting down playing with my toys, Johnny is standing over me screaming his head off, and Dad is standing off to the side trying his best to keep from laughing out loud.

Johnny was upset because his feet were cut out from under him, and *he never saw it coming.*

* * * * *

We live in troubling times. The scripture declares in Second Timothy 3:1 that perilous times are coming. If there ever was a time that seems to fit that description, it is today.

Particularly troubling to the Christian's heart is the *world situation*. With the breakup of the Soviet Union and the end of the Cold War, it seemed that eminent danger of war was over. Yet we have found there are still wars popping up that can pull American troops into dangerous situations. There is also the very real danger of nuclear weapons falling into the hands of terrorists or a madman of the type of Saddam Hussein. The illusion of peace is very fragile indeed.

Even more distressful, however, is the current condition of our own country. It seems every value we hold dear is under assault by the very nation we love. Immorality and perversion are touted as normal, and if anyone takes a stand for morality and sanity, they are labeled moral bigots. Our society has also tried to keep any vestige of Christianity or Jesus Christ out of the public view, saying it has no place in the public schools or the workplace. It is rapidly approaching the time when the greatest crime in America will be that of being a Christian.

Not only is the world generally in lousy shape, we also have to deal with stress every day of our lives. We live in such a high tech, fast-paced world that stress seems to be a constant factor that must be dealt with. On the job, there is the constant pressure to produce results in a very limited time frame. You are required to give your job first priority in your life. Job security and loyalty are nil. The threat of losing your job and being unemployed is a constant danger.

Add to this the need to balance a family life and then stress levels can go off the chart. Balancing work and family is no easy matter.

These things combine together to literally vex our very souls, leaving us disturbed and troubled. As worrisome as they are, however, most folks with varying degrees of success accept these things as a part of life. Some people cope with it all fairly well. Some people do not cope well at all but are in the process of dealing with it. Then just about the time we think we have a handle on things, something happens. WE ARE CAUGHT BY SURPRISE!

The unexpected incident can be the most troubling of all worries because you do not see it coming, and you have no way to prepare for it.

In the little story I told at the beginning of this chapter, what was it about getting tackled that upset my brother so? To begin with, *his image of himself* contributed to his anger. In his own mind, he was running around, over, and through any and all challengers to score touchdowns amid the cheers of the crowd. In his play world, he was invincible. All of a sudden, he was brought down, and it annoyed him greatly.

He was also agitated by *the size of what brought him down*. I was the little brother. He was much bigger. There was no way I should have been able to bring him down.

When we are caught by surprise, the same thoughts will plague us. We have created in our minds an image of ourselves and our strength. We feel we are on firm footing. Then, when we are knocked off our feet unexpectedly, we take a good look at what it was that tripped us up and find it was something seemingly small that caught us off guard. We will say, like Johnny did, "There's no way that should have tackled me for real." Yet it is very real, for we are on the ground.

Johnny was also disturbed by *the source* of his downfall. I think anyone in the entire neighborhood could have slipped up on Johnny, and it would not have upset him nearly as bad. But I was his brother, and that was almost more than he could stand. Perhaps the most painful of all unexpected setbacks is when it comes from a trusted friend or confidant. We expect to be hit by those who openly oppose us, but it is much different when someone we care about gives us the royal shaft. It is not the mistreatment that hurts near as much as who it is that does it.

The first casualty of our distress will be the joy we have in living—the ecstasy of simply being alive and enjoying life. Because of worry, we will not experience contentment in our lives. Instead, everything will feel "out of sorts."

There is the tendency in every generation to feel like the problems in their generation are greater than ever before. They say, "My father's generation never experienced the pressure mine does." Indeed, it seems as if the closer we get to the coming of our Lord, the more intense the fury of our adversary. With advanced technology in the hands of fallen sinners, coupled by the population explosion, the force of wickedness is intensified.

The times, however, are more perilous *only* in the sense of their intensity. Human nature remains the same. There has always been temptation to tantalize and entice men, but now there is merely more opportunity to fall. The heart of man remains the same; it houses the same human tendencies the disciples had two thousand years ago. The same things that troubled their hearts are the same things that trouble ours. If we take a close look at what was disturbing the disciples in the Upper Room, we will find something of a kinship with them.

While Jesus was speaking to his disciples, they became troubled and discomforted. What he was saying flat tore them out of the frame. SOMETIMES THE WORDS OF OUR LORD ARE UNSETTLING. We make a mistake if we think that going to church and hearing the Word of God is only supposed to make us feel good. I've even heard Christians criticize because the service wasn't "uplifting" enough. The truth is sometimes the Word of God is uncomfortable because it reveals an area of shortcoming in us. God's Word may be designed to expose our sin or to shake us out of our comfort zone and stir us to action.

The words of Jesus struck five troublesome areas in the disciples' hearts. They are the same areas we will have difficulty with.

They Were Troubled by the Prospect of Their Own Failure

If there was one thing Peter was sure of, it was in his own ability to stand. Peter's problem was not the problem of a lack of confidence. In fact, this was one of Peter's strengths. He loves Jesus and would stand by him, no matter what. He just knew he would.

He was so convinced of this that he looked Jesus in the face and said, "Lord, I will even die for you. Even if all these others should run, I will stand by your side."

Peter still had not dealt with the problem of his pride that we saw in chapter 3. He is about to get a crash course in humility.

Jesus's answer to him was, "Peter, will you really die for me? This very night, before the cock crows, you will deny that you know me three times."

One can only imagine the effect of those words on Peter's heart. They, no doubt, cut deep. "Who, me? I am the strong one. Do you mean *I* will fail?" That was exactly what Jesus was saying. He was inferring that Peter would fall *in his strong area.* The prospect of Peter failing the Lord tore his heart to pieces.

Most of us, similarly, have a high view of our own strengths. In our hearts and minds, we want to serve the Lord Jesus. We would never want to fail him. We may even recognize our weak areas and guard them closely but take for granted and leave unguarded what we consider our strong areas. It is there, at the unguarded strength, that Satan attacks. It is there that we become vulnerable.

When we realize just how easily we can fall victim to the adversary, it is truly distressing. How could I have failed to witness to that one when I had such a marvelous opportunity? How could I have reacted with such anger and hurt someone I love? How could I have thought such a thing? Or maybe we say, "How could I have yielded to temptation? I didn't want to commit that sin."

We have to realize that if any one of us takes our eyes off the Lord Jesus, we are capable of falling. A few days without spending time with the Lord, a little while without reading his Word and praying, and we leave ourselves unguarded. Then the right circumstances arise, and we find ourselves staring temptation in the face. The ease with which our frail human nature can fail the Lord is shocking. The purest saint a few steps away from the Lord can act like the vilest sinner.

When we realize just how we are, that we have clay feet, it blows our self-image of strength out of the water.

Thank God through his strength we can stand faithful. Praise God for his merciful, forgiving nature. If, however, we forget we are dependent on him and try to stand on our own, we are bound to fall.

Peter, when confronted by the possibility of his own failure, was troubled in his heart.

THEY WERE TROUBLED BY THE FAILURES OF OTHERS

In the view of the disciples, Jesus made one of the most shocking predictions imaginable in the Upper Room. After he had taught them humility by his own example, the Bible says he became troubled in spirit. He then spoke words that were like an exploding bomb. "One of you shall *betray* me."

Nothing could have caused a bigger commotion among the disciples than this statement. As they each one began to ask "Is it I?" their confusion only deepened. We might better understand their question as "You're not talking about me, are you?" Perhaps they felt Jesus had misinterpreted some action of theirs. Certainly no one in this band of men would actually betray Jesus.

We have a tendency to look at this scene from the standpoint of knowing what Judas is about to do. We view Judas as a suspicious, sinister figure most folks would have mistrusted. The truth is however dark his heart might have been, on the outside, he seemed the paragon of virtue. No one suspected Judas. He held the confidence of the disciples. No one, save Jesus, knew what was in his heart.

For three years, these men had close fellowship together. They had forsaken all, followed Jesus, and invested their very lives in his claims. They had seen his power displayed in the many miracles he performed. They had even seen his power at work in their own lives when Jesus sent them out and gave them authority over the demon possessed.

Their bond had been forged in the fires of opposition and tribulation. In spite of their squabbles they felt they were united in a common cause, striving for a common goal. Now Jesus is saying one of their group is going to betray him.

As they began to look around the room, never suspecting Judas, they began to wonder and question who it was that Jesus was speaking about. Is it any wonder they were upset? The prospect of one of their own, whom they loved dearly, failing the Lord troubled them deeply.

In the past few years, we have seen several high profile preachers fall into sin, and it has been distressful. Since they were such well-recognized names, it was splashed across the newspapers. The response from the world was "See, they're all a bunch of hypocrites." I personally have heard people say that, and probably, so have you. What is especially disconcerting about it is the way they generalize and group all Christians in the same category.

What is *heartbreaking* is the world in its wickedness will judge the claims of our precious Lord Jesus by the actions of those who claim his name. Can you imagine sinful man judging a holy God?

I have also had some personal friends I had a lot of confidence in plunge into sin. These were people I loved dearly, and it did hurt.

The unfortunate victim in these circumstances is the young Christian who has become a follower of one of these men. When they fell, the immature became disillusioned, and their faith was shaken. We must keep in mind all human beings have imperfections, and we should never follow a man. If we are truly keeping our eyes on Christ, something like this may disturb us, but it should not shake our faith. We should say, "Even if *everybody* falls, by God's grace, I'm going to continue to follow Jesus."

Just like the disciples, the actions of others can trouble us.

THEY WERE TROUBLED BECAUSE THINGS WEREN'T AS THEY EXPECTED

Things were not working out the way the disciples envisioned them. They had a preconceived notion of what the Messiah would be like and what he would accomplish. They, like many at that time, expected a political leader to break the bonds of Rome. They expected *all Israel* to enthrone him. What they saw in Jesus was something quite different.

Think with me for a few minutes about this. *The disciples are on an emotional roller coaster.* Just a few days earlier, Jesus had told them they were about to go to Jerusalem. They immediately began to question Jesus's decision. "Are you sure this is a good idea? It was just recently that they tried to kill you." But Jesus was unwavering on this point. They *were* going to Jerusalem. So positive were they that nothing good would come of it all that Thomas said, "Well, boys, let's go die with him." They started the trip in apprehension.

Along the way, something happened, however. As they began to approach Jerusalem, word spread that Jesus was coming. The closer they got to Jerusalem, the more the excitement began to build. The crowd frenzy reached a fever pitch as Jesus approached the Mount of Olives. Just over the hill was the temple mount in Jerusalem. The crowd went wild. They began to spread their coats and palm leaves in front of the donkey Jesus was riding. Spontaneously, they began to shout, "Hosanna! Hosanna to the Son of David!" It was quite an emotional outpouring.

The disciples could not have been immune to it all. I am sure they were swept up in the ecstasy of the moment. They began to say within themselves, "Maybe Jesus was right. This *is* the time to enter Jerusalem. Look at how the people are receiving him. Maybe now is the time he is going to set up his kingdom. This is it! He's going to claim his throne!" They were caught up in the emotional surge.

As they topped the Mount of Olives, they caught a panoramic view of the temple, all Jerusalem, and the surrounding hills. The vista, coupled with the rejoicing crowd, was quite intoxicating.

But then something happened. Jesus began to weep and say, "Oh, Jerusalem, Jerusalem! If you had only known the things that contribute to your peace, but you would not have me!" He then predicted the destruction of the city. With a few short words, their hopes were dashed. They in turn had been apprehensive, swept up in joy, and now thrown down to despair and disappointment.

Now as they sit around the table, the things that have transpired have left them confused. *Things were not working out as they expected them to.*

Often we have our own agendas, and we know exactly how God ought to work things out in our lives. We pray with a preset notion of how God will answer our prayer. When he does not answer *the way we want him to*, we become discouraged.

Sometimes we will enter an endeavor, whether it is a ministry, marriage, or business venture, with unrealistic expectations. When the difficulties inherent with these things arise, we become disillusioned and say with the disciples, "This is not the way I expected it to be."

THEY WERE TROUBLED BY A LACK OF UNDERSTANDING

For some time now, Jesus had been trying to prepare his disciples for the things that were about to happen. Most of the lessons just had not sunk in. Likewise, what he was saying now did not exactly make sense to them.

Jesus told them, "I am about to go away, and where I go, you cannot follow now but you will follow later."

Peter's question was, "Why can't I follow you now?" To paraphrase, he was saying, "What are you saying, Lord? I don't understand what you mean. Why can't I follow you now? *I just don't understand.*" His failure to grasp the meaning behind Jesus's words caused Peter great dismay.

There seems to be the innate need in all of us to understand everything. We seem to want to know that every situation happens for a purpose, and we want the inside information on what that purpose is.

When the unexpected happens to us, we may say, "Lord, I've tried to stay true to you and serve you. I was only trying to do right. I just don't understand why this had to happen to me." This will not merely trouble us, but it will nearly rip our hearts out by the roots.

There are two things we need to keep in mind. First, *there are some things we will never understand in this life*. When First Corinthians 13:12 says **"now we see through a glass, darkly,"** it is not referring to this fleshly veil we see through. We do not see and understand *everything* that transpires in the spiritual realm. Job never heard the challenge Satan threw up in God's face concerning Job. He only experienced the trial. As long as we are in this flesh, we will have a limited view, but thank God, the verse in Corinthians doesn't leave us with a dark glass. It goes on to say **"but then"** when we see him "face to face; now I know in part; but then shall I know even as also I am known."

Secondly, *we do not need to understand everything*. There is something, however, that we need to do instead, but I'm getting a little ahead of myself here. We'll talk about that later when we talk about the cure that the Lord Jesus gives unto us.

THEY WERE TROUBLED BECAUSE THEY COULDN'T SEE THE WAY CLEARLY

Jesus's words had another disturbing aspect. Jesus had said, "I'm going away. You cannot follow me now, but you will follow me later." Then he added these words, "Where I go, you will know, and the way, you will know."

This brought a response from Thomas. "Lord, we don't know where you are going. How can we know the way?" We can once again paraphrase it, "*We cannot see where you are leading us*." The path they would have to take in order to follow Jesus was unclear.

Not having a clear view of where Jesus is leading us or perhaps not even knowing what God's will is for our lives can be more than unsettling. Sometimes it is downright scary. We want to feel like we have our lives all mapped out and we are right on course, within *our* time frame.

We find that sometimes the Lord leads us to an action and does not tell us where it will take us. When we cannot see where it is taking us, we feel like we have *no direction*, and we may end up questioning God.

I have been a pastor, associate pastor, youth director, and a Sunday school teacher. By far, the most asked question I receive is "How can I know God's will?" It seems to be what Christians want to know more than anything else.

Let me be quick to add that God's will is knowable. He desires to make his will known unto us, but he reveals it in his own time, not within ours. We have the assurance that he will reveal his will unto us. In fact, he is more anxious for us to know his will than we are to know it. This is what was behind Jesus's statement: "Where I go, you know, and the way, you know." The way is knowable, within God's framework.

The interim time, where we can't see his leading clearly, is perplexing, however. How do we handle that uncertainty?

As Jesus speaks to the disciples, he understands how troubling his words are to them. Therefore, out of a heart of love and compassion, Jesus gives them a word. Within it is the key or the very cure for overcoming a troubled heart. Though it is a simple concept, it is the remedy for the terrible consequences of worry.

Listen carefully. The Lord is about to speak.

The Scripture

THE CURE FOR A TROUBLED HEART

PART II

"Let not your heart be troubled: ye believe in God, believe also in me."

—John 14:1

Chapter 5

THE CURE FOR A TROUBLED HEART

PART II

THE CURE IS GIVEN

Most all of my life, my dad has been my hero. When I was a young child, he was my baseball hero. Back in the 40s, before I was born, he had played professional baseball in the minor leagues. He never made it to the majors. Somewhere along the line, he had settled down with my mom, got a job, and started raising three kids.

Although he never made it to the big show, in my mind, there could not have been a better baseball player than my dad. I can remember looking at an old scrapbook filled with old newspaper clippings my mom had kept that chronicled his playing career. I can remember the pride I felt just reading them.

He is still my hero, but now that I am older, it is for a much different reason. Much of what I am, I owe to him. He raised me and tried to instill certain values within me. He and Mom provided for the needs of all of us kids. They both loved us and were Christian examples for us to follow.

There is one lesson he taught me that he may not ever have realized I was taking notice of. It was expressed in a testimony he gave that pretty well summed up his way of viewing things.

It happened in October 1962 during the Cuban missile crisis. It was positively the scariest moment of the Cold War. President John F. Kennedy had recently been on television revealing the Soviet Union's gamble and the American response. The Soviets had placed intercontinental nuclear missiles in Cuba. Kennedy was ordering a naval blockade of the island. To many people, it seemed like nuclear war was eminent. It was a time of great fear among the American people.

I was eight years old at the time. Being a child, I did not fully comprehend the gravity of the moment. I can remember in second grade going through bomb drills where we would have to duck and cover. I was aware everyone was afraid of what would happen next. Everywhere people met, there was worried talk. Even when it was not spoken of, the pall of fear hung like a morning fog, clouding our view and constantly pressing in onus. There was something else I had noticed. If my dad was afraid, he didn't show it.

Bomb shelters were the order of the day. Our neighbors across the street had built themselves a bomb shelter, which really didn't make a lot of sense. We lived nearly under the runway of Dobbins Air Force Base. Had there been a war all the bomb shelters in the world wouldn't have done us a lick of good. We would have been "toast."

One night at church, at the height of the crisis, we were having an old fashioned "testimony meeting." My dad got up and started testifying. He probably does not remember a thing he said, but what he said made an impression on his eight-year-old son.

He began by telling about the bomb shelter our neighbors had built. He then talked about how everyone was afraid. He ended his testimony by saying, "But praise God, I'm not trusting in a bomb shelter. *I'm trusting in the Lord Jesus Christ.*"

Those words were the greatest lesson he could have ever taught me. They were of much greater value than learning how to hit a curve ball. Those words reflect the truth that Jesus had tried to teach his disciples two thousand years earlier. Within that truth is the key to how to have calm in the middle of frightening circumstances.

There *is a cure* for the troubled heart.

* * * * *

Jesus knew the effect that his words were having on his disciples. He understood that their world was crumbling around them. His prediction of the destruction of Jerusalem had struck a raw nerve. Not only was their national identity about to be crushed under the heel of Rome, but the temple, the center of their faith, would be decimated. That would be disturbing enough for anyone who loved their homeland.

When you add to that the personal revelations Jesus made about the disciples, their vexation takes on monstrous proportions. How must the disciples have felt? It is hard to imagine the magnitude of it all. They were about to lose EVERYTHING, and they were powerless to stop it.

At the moment of despair, *the heart of Jesus is moved with compassion*. He has so identified with these men that he genuinely hurts when they hurt.

This is his nature, and it is still so today. Hebrews 4:15 expresses it this way: **"For we have not an high priest which cannot be touched with the feeling of our infirmities; but was in all points tempted like as we are, yet without sin."**

No heart feels for us in our time of despair like the heart of Jesus. When we experience loss, he grieves with us. When we feel like we are all alone, he is ever present. When we feel like the odds are overwhelming against us, he fights the battle for us. He does all this because his heart is touched by our tears.

So Jesus, at the critical time of the disciples' despair, said in his heart, "I just can't leave them hanging. I must give them some words to cling to. I must give them the key to overcome their despair."

In a voice tender with compassion, Jesus spoke, **"Let not your heart be troubled: ye believe in God, believe also in me."**

Here is the key to calming the heart in chaos: *trusting in Jesus*. In making that claim, I want to point out two things about Jesus's words here.

First, I want you to notice the meaning of the word *believe*. The Greek word for *believe*, *pisteuo*, means more than merely assenting to a set of facts or a creed. It means "to rely upon." Often in the New Testament, the word *believe* is synonymous with the word *trust*. Where *pisteuo* is used, *believe* and *trust* are interchangeable. It is not enough to simply believe that there is a God. It signifies a willingness to *trust* him.

Secondly, I want you to notice the object of our trust. It is not believing in some abstract supreme being. It is very specific. Jesus said "*believe in me*." The object of this kind of trust is to be Jesus himself.

What Jesus was trying to compel the disciples to do was to rely upon him. This is the same lesson he wants us to learn. When we are faced with an upsetting circumstance, a discouraging occurrence, or a frustrating predicament, we are to *rely upon Jesus*. That is what will combat the effects of a troubled heart.

WHAT DOES IT MEAN TO TRUST?

When I got saved, I trusted Jesus. Although these were not the exact words I used, in effect, I was saying, "Lord Jesus, I'm lost, and I cannot save myself. If it is left in my hands, I will go to Hell. But you died for me, and you said you would save me if I called upon your name. I believe your Word; therefore, I am taking it out of my hands, and *I am placing it in your hands*. If you do not save me, I will go straight to Hell, but I am trusting and believing in you to do what you said."

That is what it means to trust him. It is *no longer in my hands*. There is nothing I can do to save myself. I do not have the ability to earn salvation. I have placed it in his hands. That is why it is hard for me to understand a Christian doubting his salvation. If I have trusted him, *it is out of my hands*. It is in his hands. Why should I doubt his hand?

If that is the way I trusted him for salvation, then that is the way I should trust him for *everything in my life*. No matter what the circumstance or heartache, place it in his hand. If something happens that I do not understand, I must trust him to work good within it. If I cannot see the way he is leading me, I will have to trust him that he knows what is best, and he will show me the path he has marked for me.

Let's look at a situation that is a little more difficult. Someone has told a bald-faced lie about you. They have slandered you in the worst possible way. They have struck out at you and spread their maliciousness with a gossiping tongue. How do we respond?

Human nature says "Bless God, they won't get away with that! I'll show them! I will fight back!" When we do that, we are taking things in our own hands. The situation is bound to get worse.

To be perfectly honest, trusting Jesus in this instance is not easy. We really have to overcome our natural inclinations. When someone slanders us with lies, it is best not to even answer them. Do not strike back at them. Turn it over to the Lord. *Let him fight the battle for you.* Don't be distracted from your goal. Keep on serving him. Continue reaching people for Jesus.

The bottom line is if Jesus is worthy enough to be trusted for salvation, then he is worthy enough to be trusted for everything.

WHY CAN WE TRUST HIM?

Children are so trusting. They have not grown up and experienced life to the point of disappointment yet. They have not become calloused like adults. They are completely trusting. Whatever you say, they believe. This is the type of trust Jesus asks us to bring to him: a childlike faith.

Adult experience, however, tells us to be careful with whom we trust. Our nature reacts with skepticism whenever someone says "Trust me." This cynicism is usually present because someone in our past has disappointed us. Even the optimistic, trusting person will have a streak of what he calls "realism."

Unfortunately, people bring this same reluctance to trust with them when they approach the Lord. They forget God's nature is divine, not human. Recognizing this, there is a question crying out to be asked. *Why can we trust the Lord?* Is he really any different from all the others? Can we find reassurance that he is trustworthy?

There are two main reasons why we can totally and unreservedly trust him.

The first reason is we can trust him *because of his nature*. By nature, he cannot lie. His very nature is holiness. What he says in his Word is truth. When God makes a promise and writes it down in his Word, he is honor bound to fulfill it.

Not only is he truth, but by nature, he is also love. No heart could ever be as caring as the heart of Jesus. No heart could yearn and long for us like his. As the embodiment of pure love, Jesus's desire for us is that we experience the best his will provides for us.

When the Lord allows something to come into our lives, do we really trust him? Do we believe he wants what is best for us, or do we question his working? If we truly believe in him, we will believe he wants the best for us and trust him implicitly. He is trustworthy because of his nature.

The second reason we can trust him is *because of his ability*. He is all-powerful. As El Shaddai, he is the all-sufficient one. Everything I need is wrapped up in Jesus. He has the ability to meet any need or solve any problem I have. He has the ability.

Let me illustrate this if I may.

Suppose there is a Christian brother who lives near me. This is a precious brother I have the utmost confidence in. We have had wonderful fellowship together. We have served the Lord together. There is nothing I wouldn't do for him.

Now suppose that early one morning, he knocks at my door. When I answer, it he begins to say, "Brother Jimmy, I really need help. My car absolutely will not start, and I have no money to call a mechanic. If I don't make it to a meeting, I'm in serious trouble. Can you help me?"

Being the good neighbor that I am, I pop the hood of his car and stare blankly at the engine. What you have got to understand is you could take everything I know about a car engine and, maybe, fill a paragraph. I don't have a clue as to what the car needs in order to be fixed.

I say to myself then, "I know what I'll do. I'll pay for either a mechanic to fix his car or a taxi to take him to the meeting." So I pull out my bank book and discover to my dismay that I have no money either.

My final option is to take him to the meeting myself. When I try to start my truck of all things, it will not start either. Now we are really in a fix.

In my heart, I know my brother has a need, and I really want to help him. What I have to say, however, is, "I'm sorry, my friend. I cannot help you." My heart feels for his predicament, but I do not have the ability to help him. It is something out of my power.

That may be a simplistic illustration, but it does demonstrate the limitations of human abilities. There will be times when a friend may be having all sorts of emotional or spiritual problems, and all of your stock answers do not seem to help. You want to help them, but you are limited by surface understanding.

Praise God, it is not that way with the Lord. Not only is his character such that he wants the best for his children but *he has all power* as well. He is sufficient for every spiritual, emotional, or physical need we have. He has the answer when I do not. He has the ability to meet that need. In fact, he is all I need.

He can be trusted because of his *nature* and because of his *ability*.

HOW DOES TRUSTING CURE A TROUBLED HEART?

It may seem strange that a Christian would overlook something as basic as trusting Jesus, but we do have a bad tendency to overlook the obvious. Even when confronted with the promises of scripture, we find a little bit of "doubting Thomas" in us. We find ourselves asking the question, "*How* does that work? What does trusting do for an individual? How can trusting Jesus cure a troubled heart?"

The first effect that trusting has on us is *it negates worry*.

A person who worries about everything has a time bomb ticking inside him. He keeps building up anxiety, which at some point is bound to explode.

Worry has dire effects on all of us. It affects you emotionally, physically, and spiritually. It affects you physically in that it can literally make you sick. It can cause ulcers and hair loss, and the resultant stress can contribute to heart problems. If affects you emotionally by keeping you in a constantly stressed-out condition. You then find yourself lashing out at those around you. It affects you spiritually in that it causes you to rely upon your own ingenuity to solve problems instead of placing it in his hands. There is the constant fretting, "I've got to find a solution for this."

Trusting Jesus sweeps this worry away. We realize we don't have to "sweat the details." We are literally living by faith. This type of trust shows a *confidence* in our Lord. We are confident in his leading. We are confident he will show us his will. We just know he will only allow what is being in our lives. We may not understand it all, but we just have confidence in him. In fact, we are commanded in Philippians 4:6 to **be anxious for nothing**.

The second way trusting calms us is *it places the problem in more capable hands than ours.*

We place a high premium on being independent and self-sufficient. In many ways, this can be considered a virtue. We have to be responsible enough to earn our own living. A mature adult does not desire to be supported by others. He makes his own way, accepting the responsibility for his actions and striving to better himself. This is an admirable quality.

The problem comes when we let that independence extend into our relationship with the Lord. When a difficulty arises, we jump right in feet first and begin to try and work things out. We just know we are capable to solve it, and we rely on all of our intellectual resources to arrive at a solution. It is a rude awakening when we discover we are insufficient to handle some things or that we handle them very badly.

When I trust Jesus and place it all in his hands, I am taking the problem out of my imperfect hands and placing them into hands much more capable of handling things. Doing this does not mean I am abdicating responsibility or doing nothing. It is simply the wisest possible move I can make.

When I have demonstrated this kind of reliance in the Lord, there is no room for worry. I have the utmost confidence in his leading, and I'm not fretting over the consequences. I have placed it in all-powerful hands. The same hands that made me now hold my destiny. What calm and peace there is in knowing I am in capable hands.

That brings us to the third effect trusting has on us. *It allows the peace of God to rule our lives.*

Did you realize that allowing peace to rule our lives IS A CONSCIOUS CHOICE WE MAKE? The scripture bears this out. **"And let the peace of God rule in your hearts, to which also you were called in one body; and be thankful"** (Col. 3:15, NKJV). When our lives are in chaos, it means we have allowed something to rob us of our peace. We can choose chaos or we can choose to have God's peace.

Trusting Jesus allows God to saturate your heart with peace in a very supernatural way. We won't go into detail at this point. We will deal in depth with having the peace of God in a later chapter.

GOD'S RESPONSE TO FAITH

Faith provokes a response from God. When he sees one of his children going through a trial with their faith remaining strong, it strikes a chord in the heart of God. He does not leave his child comfortless. He reacts.

The first reaction from God is he is pleased. *Faith pleases God.* When there seems to be no reason to sing yet he sees his child singing, he is pleased. When temptation raises its venomous head and the Christian continues to stand strong, it brings satisfaction to the heart of the Father.

The scripture states that **"without faith it is impossible to please him"** (Heb. 11:6, NKJV).

Can you imagine that? I have it within my power to please the Creator of the universe. A Christian can live a life of faith and thereby bring pleasure to the heart of God.

I often fall short in the faith department, but I know my heart I want to please my Father. After all the Lord has done for me, pleasing him ought to be the driving force in my life.

God's next response is *he takes a bad situation and begins to work good out of it.* Whereas we cannot see anything of value in difficulties, God sees them as the building blocks of character.

God may be using the natural difficulties of life to instill strength or impart values to us. I have been saved for fifty-three years at the time of this writing. I have been preaching for over forty years. Looking back over that time, I have come to the realization that if I have any spiritual strength, if I have any insight concerning spiritual matters, it was developed during my times of trial. During those low moments when I couldn't see his hand, God was working a marvelous work in my life. I thank God for the tests that have come my way.

The work he does is accomplished within us. He takes the events in our lives and *begins to conform us to the image of his Son.* He is shaping and molding us our entire lives.

"And we know that all things work together for good to them that love God, to them who are the called according to his purpose. For whom he did foreknow, he also did predestinate to be conformed to the image of his Son, that he might be the first-born among many brethren" (Rom. 8:28–29).

Even as I am writing this, my heart is uttering a prayer. Oh Lord, chip away anything in my life that is unlike you. Let me be clay in your hands. Make me what you desire me to be.

After we have placed our trust in him, *he confirms his word in our hearts.* He gives us something *to support our faith.*

As we shall see in the next chapter, Jesus gave them the cure for a troubled heart, then he gave them some words of encouragement to strengthen and give support to their faith.

Whatever may be troubling or disturbing your soul, a cure may be found in the mercies of Jesus.

Are you, like Peter, experiencing the guilt that accompanies falling into sin? Have you failed the Lord? The good news is there is forgiveness for our sins. **"If we confess our sins, he is faithful and just to forgive us our sins, and to cleanse us form all unrighteousness"** (1 John 1:9).

Are you disillusioned by the failure of others? Don't focus on all those around you. Keep your eyes on the one who will not fail you. He is the one we trust, not frail humans.

Are things not working out the way you expected them to? Do you cry out, "Lord, I don't understand?" Is the path you are walking unclear and you are unable to see where it is leading you?

He made you the way you are. He knows what is best suited for you. *You can trust him.*

> **"Trust in the LORD with all thine heart; and lean not unto thine own understanding. In all thy ways acknowledge him, and he shall direct thy paths"**
>
> —(Prov. 3:5–6).

The Scripture
WORDS OF ENCOURAGEMENT

"In my Father's house are many mansions: if it were not so, I would have told you. I go to prepare a place for you. And if I go and prepare a place for you, I will come again, and receive you unto myself; that where I am, there ye may be also."

—John 14:2–3

Chapter 6

WORDS OF ENCOURAGEMENT

There's an old story about a little old lady who loved the Lord Jesus. The story is older than I am, and I have no idea where I heard it for the first time.

This precious lady was in her eighties. She had received the Lord Jesus at a very early age and had lived a long fruitful life. Years before, her husband had passed away. Most of her close friends had also gone on. She had taught Sunday school for years but was now too feeble to do much. Her time was spent going to church, praying for her pastor, and worrying over her grandchildren.

She had a grandson who was something of a skeptic. He was a very "enlightened" young man who, unfortunately, felt like he was too intelligent and sophisticated to believe in Granny's old ways.

One day, during a visit while they were sitting on her front porch, they got into a very lively discussion about the things of God. With a very sarcastic attitude, the grandson began to question all the things she believed in.

"Granny," he said, "you're all the time talking about praying. Your answer to everything is let's pray about it. When you could be accomplishing something with your time, all you say is pray, pray,

pray. That doesn't accomplish anything. It's just words in the air—a total waste of time."

"Well," she replied, "if there's nothing to it, then you won't mind if I continue to pray for you, will you? I would really like to see you get saved so I could see you in Heaven someday."

"This business about getting saved just isn't rational. It is all so subjective. You say Jesus lives in your heart. How can you know that?"

"It's like this, son," she began. "You see this house I live in? I live here all alone. You can't tell me a boarder could move into one of these rooms, and I wouldn't know it. There would be some signs he was here. I'd find some dirty clothes that weren't mine or some dirty dishes I didn't mess up. There would be some evidence he was here. When Jesus moved into my heart, there was a change. There was evidence he was there."

Undaunted, the young man continued. "All right, let's reason this thing out. How do you know there's a Heaven?"

"Because Jesus said there was."

"Is that the only reason you can come up with?"

"No," she calmly replied. "Sometimes in this world, I can kind of catch a little breeze from that shore. There are times in church when God begins to move that it seems like a little bit of Haeaven is blowing through our midst. Sometime when I'm sitting out here on this porch, reading my Bible and thinking about some of my friends who have gone on, a small, heavenly breeze starts stirring."

The frustration was beginning to get to him. "Let's make a supposition here. You've spent all your life believing this stuff. What if one day you die, and there is no Heaven? What then? You've wasted your life."

The young man was smugly thinking, "I've got her now. There's no way she can answer that."

The old lady studied about it for a while. She then looked up at her grandson and began to speak. "That's a good question. The only thing I can say to you is I know there is a Heaven. But suppose you are right. I'd still be a Christian. *There's so much Heaven on the way to Heaven that I'd be a Christian even if there were no Heaven.*"

* * * * *

"Give us proof!"

This is the demand the skeptical world presents to the child of God. They live in an unstable world that is so unpredictable they see nothing as absolute. There are thousands of voices calling out to them offering their particular brand of philosophy. Is it any wonder the unbeliever's life is filled with uncertainty?

Along comes the Christian who dogmatically states there is only one way to eternal life, and it is found in Jesus Christ. The unbeliever reacts with cynicism to such an unqualified statement. "How do you know you are right and the other person is wrong?" he asks. "Can you show me you are right? Where is your proof?"

Is there proof? Is there a way to take a scientific or mathematical formula and prove the existence of God?

We can see his handiwork. Creation attests to the existence of God, but there is not enough of a revelation of God in nature to let man know who God is and how we can know him. It merely shows us the byproducts of a great designer but does not show us him.

The Christian life is not a matter of proof or walking by sight. It is a matter of *faith*. **"Through faith we understand that the worlds were framed by the word of God, so that the things which are seen were not made of things which do not appear"** (Heb. 11:3).

Furthermore, faith does not *require* proof. **"Now faith is the substance** (or the confidence) **of things hoped for, the evidence of things not seen"** (Heb. 11:1, emphasis added). It would take no faith to believe something that could be seen.

God *does* give the Christian, however, a word of assurance he can rest in. This is how it works.

Before I got saved, *there was no proof* there was a God or that he could deliver me from my sins. There was the moving of the Holy Spirit taking the Word of God and drawing me to the point of conviction, but quite apart from proof, I received him *by faith*.

After I received him by faith, an amazing thing happened. The Holy Spirit came to live within my heart and *confirmed* within my heart his existence. Romans 8:16 testifies to this when it says that

"the Spirit itself beareth witness with our spirit that we are the children of God." *That was all the proof I needed.*

Before I was saved, there was no proof. When I got saved, he confirmed his word within me. This is the way God works. He never leaves us without assurance. He always gives us *something to confirm our faith.*

This is exactly what Jesus did for the disciples in the Upper Room. After he gave them instruction on trusting him, he gave them some words of encouragement. First came the cure, then came the confirmation.

These words were meant to be supports for their faith. They were to act as consolation for the disciples. They were promises they could cling to whenever they were facing a test. Even today, these words can bring comfort to the heart of God's child and encourages him to continue in the battle.

Much of the rest of what Jesus said in the Upper Room were words of encouragement, with a little instruction along the way. Much of the rest of this book, then, will deal with the encouragement we need or the perceptions we have that need adjusting. There will be some instruction sprinkled in to help us as we learn how to trust him. Life, after all, is a learning experience.

With that in mind, let's take a look at Jesus's objective in speaking these words and then examine the actual words themselves.

THE TEMPORAL VERSUS THE ETERNAL

Jesus's objective was to get their focus off those temporal circumstances and place them on those things that are eternal. When we are going through a trial, we usually get bogged down with temporal things—things that are going to pass away. Instead of letting these problems fill our focus to the point of despair, we should *view them in the light of eternity.*

Viewing things form an eternal perspective will do two things for us. First, it *sheds new light* on the problems we are facing. It might show us just how insignificant our difficulty is. Too often, the problem upsetting us so is something minor that we have totally blown out of proportion. We have made it much larger than it should be. Seeing them from a heavenly viewpoint shows just how small the problem actually is. The dilemma we are facing, just like everything else temporal, will pass away.

Secondly, viewing things from an eternal perspective lets us *see what is actually important in life*. Are the activities we are involved in affecting the temporal, or are they making an impact on eternity? We have to spend a great deal of time making a living. That is necessary. Outside of that, how much of our time is spent on what is passing away, and how much time do we devote to the service of God, which will last forever?

There's an old saying I really don't care for. You've heard it said before that someone was so "heavenly minded he was of no earthly good." I am convinced the person who has his mind on heavenly matters will accomplish more on this earth than the man who is totally wrapped up in the mundane things of life. How can a man catch a glimpse of God, get a feel of his heart, partake in his nature, and *not* be moved with compassion for the plight of man?

When faced with a trial, do not let it consume your life. View it from Heaven's standpoint, then maybe you will be able to see that God is at work in the situation. It will also take your eyes off yourself and allow you to see others around you. Then you will be able to serve God and mankind in the midst of your test.

THE EXISTENCE OF HEAVEN AS THE HOME OF THE SAINTS

In trying to encourage his disciples, Jesus gave them some of the most comforting words ever spoken. **"In my Father's house are many mansions: if it were not so I would have told you. I go to prepare a place for you"** (verse 2). What do these words tell us about the Father's house?

These words tell us that *Heaven is a real locality*. It was not something made up by men to try and fulfil an emotional need as the world would have you think. It is a place just as real as the world we are living in now. Since these words came from the lips of Jesus, we have assurance of their truthfulness.

During this time of adversity, which the disciples were entering, Jesus wanted to confirm in their hearts that Heaven was not a mere dream. It was home. In effect, what Jesus was saying to them was, "I am not deceiving you. If this were not so, don't you think I would have been honest and told you?"

For thousands of years, innumerable Christians have found hope in this thought. When the cruel world seemed to be getting the best of them, they rejoiced in the idea that this world was not their home. They were citizens of another world, merely passing as strangers through this land. How many of these pilgrims, when facing the death of a loved one, have encouraged themselves in these words, believing there is a better place their loved one has gone to?

How could a brief twenty-five-word assertion hold such an emotional grip and sway the thinking of so many for so long? It is because the Spirit of the Living God has taken the words of scripture and testified to their truthfulness. Heaven is not a fantasy. It is as real as this place I live in now. Just as sure as I breathe air here, I will one day step on that shore and catch a fresh breath, a cool and refreshing breath, of Heaven's atmosphere.

These words also tell us Heaven is *the home of a family.* The house belongs to the Father, and the Father has numerous children. All those who are part of God's family who are his children through the new birth have a place there.

There is something very special about "family." No bond is quite as close. We are related by blood. We may even have difficulties with each other, but when one family member is assailed by someone outside the family circle, the loving family pulls itself together in support of that one.

That is the way it should be with the family of God. We too are related by blood—the shed blood of Jesus Christ. There is a bond between brothers and sisters in Christ that should not be easily broken. We share the same Father. When we are following Christ, we share the same vision and the same goal. We are partakers together of the divine nature. We have the same hope. This is why I can go to preach at another church and be among people I have never met before but still feel closeness and a bond with these people. It is because they are "family."

As family, we have a home—a place we are destined to share together. Can you imagine the marvelous fellowship we will enjoy with our family there? Can you picture the friends we have served with, fellowshipped with, and cried with all gathered together rejoicing in the presence of the Lord? I've got to believe one of the joys of Heaven will be seeing our Christian friends and sharing together how the Lord delivered us.

We also see in this passage that *it is a large house*. It contains **many mansions** (literally, many dwelling places). There is room for all of God's children, from the greatest to the very least. Not one is left out. It does not tax God to find a place for us. As his nature is to give in abundance, so his house, with all its dwelling places, is so vast and so grand as to defy all human descriptions, and we can refer to them only as "mansions."

Lastly, we see that *it is a prepared place*. It is being prepared by the very hand of our Lord Jesus himself. It is hard to imagine all that Heaven holds for us. We have descriptions of it in God's Word, but to try and grasp it all is beyond our finite imagination.

Even if we cannot conceive in our feeble minds all that makes up Heaven, CONSIDER THE HAND THAT IS PREPARING IT. It is the same hand that touched the blind man and restored his sight. It is the same hand that stretched over a stormy sea, calming the raging waters and bringing peace. It is the same hand that after giving itself to be nailed to a cross, snatched up the key to death and Hell and, with a thunderous voice, proclaimed, "If a man believes in me, though he were dead, YET SHALL HE LIVE!"

It is the same hand that took a Hell-bound sinner and, by the strength of that hand, cleaned him up and began to reshape a horrible mess into a life of beauty. When you consider what we have seen that hand do, is it any wonder what he is preparing for us there is far beyond our abilities to describe?

After giving the disciples these encouraging words, he then made them a promise.

THE PROMISES OF CHRIST'S RETURN FOR HIS CHILDREN

Much of what Jesus had been saying the past couple of weeks had been intended as a *preparation of the disciples* for what was about to happen. He was going to leave them. As disturbing as those words were, he wanted to spare them the shock of a sudden loss.

The more he tried to prepare them for his leaving, however, the less they wanted to hear. They had developed that unique ability called "selective hearing." They heard what they wanted to hear. For the next few days, they would be so blinded by their sorrow that they would not be able to see God's hand was working in the very circumstances that had them so upset.

What the disciples did not comprehend was there was an essential *purpose for his leaving*. Jesus was about to PURCHASE FOR HIMSELF A PEOPLE. By dying on a cross, he would purchase salvation for as many as would believe. He would gather for himself a new breed of people—washed in the blood, born-again children.

He would then conquer death, ascend to the Father, and there PRESENT HIS BLOOD on the altar of Heaven saying, "Father, this blood is for the redemption of the nations." That blood he presented is the only reason I can gain access to Heaven when I die. It is the only credential I can show that I have inherited eternal life.

As we have already covered, he left to PREPARE A PLACE for us. He had said he was going to prepare a place "for you." One built specifically for his own and built with us in mind.

While he was gone, he would be seated at the right hand of the Father to PLEAD OUR CASE. He is there making intercession for us. When one of his children falter and an accusation is brought against him by the adversary, Jesus points to the blood he has presented and cries, "Show mercy, Father! He is one of mine!" When a follower of his is exhausted, discouraged, and at the end of his strength, Jesus says, "Father, that one needs strength and a word of encouragement. He is one of mine!" He is actively making intercession for us even this very moment.

So his purpose for leaving can be described as four *P's*. He left to purchase, present, prepare, and plead.

But he didn't just leave them hanging. He left them with his *promise to return*. He told them leaving was necessary but that **"if I go and prepare a place for you, I will come again, and receive you unto myself; that where I am, there ye may be also"** (verse 3).

What a comfort we can find in these words! Do you feel like you are facing a hostile world that would like to sacrifice you on their altar of ambition? Take heart! This world is not home, and he's coming to remove us from these hostile environs. Are you tired and exhausted, feeling like you're serving him all alone? Strengthen yourself with this thought: He is coming back to gather you together with all of his servants.

Do you long to see the face of Jesus? One day, you will not have to see him strictly with an eye of faith. He will step out over the earth and call you by name. You'll be caught up in a rapture of joy and swept into his presence. There, what you have looked upon by faith you will then view in plain sight. Together we will drink in the beauty of that face and, in overwhelming ecstasy, cry out, "My Lord and my God! Thou art all together lovely. Thou art worthy to reign!"

One of the most wonderful aspects about his coming is the fact that it is PERSONAL. He is coming in person to receive us personally. He told the disciples, "I am coming to **receive you**." Let me make a bold statement here. Of all the promises in God's word (which are all 100 percent accurate), nothing is surer than this promise. Why do I say that? It is because he is coming back to get something very valuable to the heart of God. He is returning for his prized possession—the church.

If that isn't blessed enough, I want you to notice with whom we will PARTNER. Jesus said, "I am coming to receive you **unto myself; that where I am, there ye may be also**." At his coming, we will be taken away to the marriage supper of the Lamb—there to be eternally joined with the Lord Jesus.

Can you imagine forever being in the presence of Jesus? Can you envision having fellowship with the one who made us, died for us, saved us, and fought our battles? If in this life, he at times floods us with such joy, then the joy in his very presence must be overwhelming. It is no wonder we will need a new glorified body. This one wouldn't be able to take it.

What is going to make Heaven so wonderful? The Bible tells us the street of that city is made of gold so pure that it is transparent. Each gate is made of a single giant pearl. It will be a wonder to behold, but those things will not make it wonderful. It is going to be wonderful because Jesus is there, and we will be with him. Wherever Jesus is, it will be Heaven.

For much of my young Christian life, and even into my early years of ministry, I concentrated on living the Christian life in this world. I have always loved life, and I tried to emphasize the abundance of joy in this life. I believed in and preached on Heaven, but I rarely thought about it. Someday I would go there, but I was young and had an entire life to serve Jesus. It seldom crossed my mind.

I *still* love life and hope to live a very long time, but I have found the older I get, there is a deep-seated yearning within me, born by the Spirit of God, to see his face as I step into another world. The only way I can describe it is a desire to see *home*.

The more I see of this world and its cruelty, the more I agree with the Apostle Paul that **"if in this life only we have hope in Christ, we are of all men most miserable"** (1 Cor. 15:19).

Are you facing a test? Are you exhausted by the daily strain? Take your eyes off this temporal sphere. This is not home. We are not children of this world. We have a blessed hope beyond these puny trials. There all these pressing problems will melt into insignificance as we enter the presence of the one who bought us with his blood. Rest in him.

The Scripture

SEEING THE FATHER

"Thomas saith unto him, Lord, we know not whither thou goest; and how can we know the way?

Jesus saith unto him, I am the way, the truth, and the life: no man cometh unto the Father, but by me. If ye had known me, ye should have known my Father also: and from henceforth ye know him, and have seen him.

Philip saith unto him, Lord, show us the Father, and it sufficeth us.

Jesus saith unto him, Have I been so long time with you, and yet hast thou not known me, Philip? He that hath seen me hath seen the Father; and how sayest thou then, Shew us the Father? Believest thou not that I am in the Father, and the Father in me? The words that I speak unto you I speak not of myself: but the Father that dwelleth in me, he doeth the works. Believe me that I am in the Father, and the Father in me: or else believe me for the very works' sake."

—John 14:5–11

Chapter 7

SEEING THE FATHER

Let's try and use our imagination. Imagine you are living in Bethlehem before the birth of Christ. In order to do this, you must lift yourself out of the church age, place yourself in a completely different dispensation, and view life from the vantage point of that age instead of our own.

Picture a couple named Elnathan and Miriam. Place yourself in their shoes.

Elnathan is a shepherd. Your name means "God the giver." You tend flocks around Jerusalem, basically earning your livelihood the same way as your father and his father and his father before him. Much of the flock, which you pasture outside of Bethlehem, will be used in the temple sacrifices, affording you a slight profit. Even though your name reflects a giving God, you have had to work hard all your life, and you feel like very little has been "given" to you.

Because you are a shepherd, you are looked down upon by others. Let's face it. Shepherds don't have that great a reputation for honesty or morality. In fact, you would not be able to give testimony at the gate because the testimony of a shepherd is not considered reliable. While there are many cases where this would ring true, you resent being lumped together in that group.

The name Miriam means "obstinate." You barely knew this man when you were given to him in marriage at the age of sixteen. You have since bore him four children. Your life is difficult. While Elnathan tends the flock, you tend the children, prepare all the meals for this family, make sufficient clothing for everyone, take care of a very humble dwelling, and handle countless other crises that arise. This is "expected" of you. Your life is characterized by drudgery, and you feel it is all just meaningless existence. Elnathan is a good enough man, and you suppose you love him. But things are not always good between the two of you, and you don't feel like he really understands your restlessness.

You have one joy in life. That is your infant son, Jonathan. Your three eldest children are all girls, and you love them dearly. But like the typical Israelite that you are, you and Elnathan see Jonathan as the one who will perpetuate your name.

Together you have seen the greed and corruption that runs through the temple sacrifice system. As one who provides lambs to those who would sell them to travel-weary pilgrims for a profit, Elnathan has seen the fallacies inherent in the arrangement.

You can list the things that have gone wrong with the entire setup. The sacrifice calls for a spotless lame with no blemish on it. You know for a fact that some lame or sickly specimens have been passed off on desperate travelers who have no choice but to take them. You have seen the inflated pricing, especially during holy seasons. When Jews from other countries came to Jerusalem and needed to exchange their currency, you have seen the unfair exchange rate that in effect charges interest for the privilege of exchanging their money. And lastly, you have seen the priests who exacted gifts for accepting the lamb to be sacrificed.

All this has affected the way you view organized religion. You still believe in God, but you have become disillusioned with all the trappings of religion.

Once again, remember you are in an entirely different dispensation. Consider these other factors that would influence your viewpoint.

You have no personal copy of scripture. You have heard it read in the synagogue, but you have never personally read it.

There has not been a real prophet of God in over four hundred years. There have been pretenders who preached revolution, but their end was swift. There has been no one thundering a message from God.

You are living in the age when the Spirit of God has not yet indwelled believers. God has never spoken personally to you. You have never sensed his presence. There has never been a stirring deep inside your soul that testified of a loving God.

All you know about God is what has been told to you.

Then one day, tragedy comes your way. Jonathan takes a fever. Your infant son, who is the apple of your eye, is hovering on the verge of death.

After tending to him and nursing him as best you can, he passes away. Where can you find comfort?

Considering all this, how could you, a frail human being, know God or understand what he is like? How could you "see" God the Father?

What would your concept of God be like?

* * * * *

Our world is filled with religion. If you were to take a poll, probably the vast majority of people in our nation would claim to be religious. The only problem is too often, their religion does not translate into their personal lives. The everyday conduct of the people in America doesn't reflect what they say they believe.

The truth is, instead of worshipping God, most people worship *their own concept of God*. They basically shape God into their own image. Regardless of what the Word of God may say about something, they reason, "Certainly God must think the way I do." Instead of trying to seek after God and know him for who he is, they will twist scripture to fit their own pre-set notions.

The big drawback in all this is when testing comes, they find no comfort in their belief. It may not be a stone idol they are worshipping, but just like a stone idol, their concept of God has no ears to hear their cry. There are no loving eyes to see their plight. There is no hand to grasp hold of. There is no strong arm to lift them up.

This leads them to the point of frustration. They sense their faith is empty, and often, they end up saying there is nothing to "faith in God" at all. They never stop to consider that maybe their very idea of God was false to begin with.

Ask yourself these questions: Am I worshipping the real thing or just my conception of God? Is there any real comfort in your faith? In the middle of a trial, have you ever found yourself saying, "Why would God allow this to happen to *me*?"

How can a sinful human being like myself, draped in the limitations of flesh, know what a holy and infinite God is like? What is God's nature?

THE DESIRE TO SEE THE FATHER

The disciples had a similar problem understanding who Jesus was and what he was all about. In their confusion, they made a request of Jesus. Let me set up the conversation that led to this request.

After telling them he was going away, Jesus said, "And where I am going you know, and the way you know."

With a bewildered look on his face, Thomas began to speak, "Lord, we have no idea where you are going. How in the world are we supposed to know the way?"

Jesus responded with some of the most profound words he ever uttered. He said, "**I am the way, the truth, and the life: no man cometh to the Father but by me.**"

This stirred something deep inside Philip, and he spoke, "Lord, let us see the Father, and we will be satisfied."

At first glance, this request seems to be born of ignorance. There's a reason for that: it was. However, do not overlook something essential here. Philip's appeal to the Lord, even though it was unlearned, does illustrate a deep desire in the soul of Philip.

Philip's desire was obviously more than just an aspiration to see the Father physically. It was a longing to see him in respect to "knowing" him. I believe it signified the desire to know God intimately and   grow in that relationship. Philip himself may not have completely understood his request, but the desire was there.

A principle of scripture is outlined in Luke 11:9–10. It asserts: **"Ask, and it shall be given you; seek, and ye shall find; knock, and it shall be opened unto you. For every one that asketh receiveth; and he that seeketh findeth; and to him that knocketh it shall be opened."**

Simply put, *God rewards the seeking heart.* A soul that in earnest desires to know God and diligently seeks after him will find what he seeks.

That holy, God-given desire is essential to receiving from the Lord. God will not burglarize the human will. He enters where he is invited.

Have you longed to see God and know him intimately? Rest in this promise: seek and ye shall find.

I have known people who would agonize and say, "I am really searching for God, but I can't seem to find him." They would live their lives in a state of depression, distraught that they never seemed to find peace of mind. Yet the scripture says "Seek and ye shall find." You may ask, "Jimmy, how do you reconcile that?"

To begin with, I don't try to reconcile what my finite mind may not understand. *I just believe the Word of God.* However, let me offer a possibility to you.

Could it possibly be that the person has a preconceived notion of God? Instead of seeking after God, could he be pursuing his own concept of God? Could he have set some "conditions" on God? Yes, he says he is seeking God, but his God has to fit into what he sees as God.

Make no mistake about it. You don't come to God on your own terms. You come to him on his terms. You don't strike a bargain with God. You come repenting of your sins.

Yes, God is a **"rewarder of them that diligently seek him"** (Heb. 11:6b). The soul that throws off all his own conditions and will come to God on God's terms will find him. **"All that the Father**

giveth me shall come to me; and him that cometh to me I will in no wise cast out" (John 6:37).

Jesus responded to Philip's desire. It may not have been what Philip was expecting, but it was the honest answer to his request.

TO "SEE" ME IS TO "SEE" THE FATHER

In the quiet of that Upper Room, Jesus makes a couple of bold assertions to his disciples. There's no denying or getting around the enormity of those claims. They are stated as absolutes.

The first claim is *Jesus is the only access to the Father.* He clearly states, "No man comes to the Father, but by me." Literally, no one can know God outside of Jesus Christ. NO one can truly worship God except through Jesus Christ. He is not merely a way—he is *the only way* to the Father. He claims absolute authority in the matter of salvation.

People don't like absolutes. They will say "I believe in God," then try to bypass his provision for their redemption. Jesus is the *way* to God, he is the eternal *truth* of God, and he is the one who infuses *life* into the dreariness of our existence.

His second claim was *"If you see me you have seen the Father."*

How can a sinful human being know what a holy God is like? In the illustration at the beginning of this chapter, how could someone like Elnathan know what the nature of God is?

Jesus was saying to them, "Whatever you see in me, you can know that it is one of the traits of God." If you want to know what God is like, look at Jesus.

It is evident that this is what the followers of Jesus understood him to mean, for they would expound upon it in the years to come. John called him the "Word" of God (John chapter 1), the very expression of the heart of God. He then states he actually *is* God. The writer of the Book of Hebrews calls him the **express image of God** (Heb. 1:3). Over and over, they assert and reassert this truth.

He literally took upon himself the flesh of men and was "God with us." Man at last could gaze upon God in the flesh and see in this one what God was like.

Within the life of Jesus, we can clearly see the nature of God.

THE TRAITS FOUND IN JESUS

We can look at Jesus and see unlimited power. We see him calming the storm, healing the sick, and casting out demons, all of which illustrate the fact that the elements, diseases, and even fallen angels are subjected to him. We see him approach a grave and thunder out the words, "Lazarus, come forth!" We watch in awe and a little bit of fear as Lazarus steps forth out that grave. The seemingly unconquerable enemy is powerless before him. In all this, we see God is a God of *infinite power.*

On numerous occasions in the Gospels, it says Jesus "knew their thoughts." He literally knew the heart of man. He was the great revealer of true motives. We know then that God is *all-knowing.*

We see Jesus as he takes little children into his arms and begins to bless them. We find assurance in the fact that our God can be *moved with compassion.*

We see Jesus as he takes a whip and begins to drive the money changers out of the temple. His zeal in driving them out tells us God *hates sin and hypocrisy.* We see Jesus approach a fig tree, find no fruit, and place a curse upon it, causing it to wither. We see illustrated in this that God is a God of *judgment.*

A woman caught in the act of adultery is brought to Jesus. Israel's law demanded she be stoned. Jesus turns the spotlight on the sin of those who brought her to him. As they drift off in shame, Jesus asks her, "Are there any left who accuse you?"

She answers, "There are none."

Even though he alone has the authority to pass judgment upon her and that judgment would be just, he instead utters some of the most precious words in scripture. "Neither do I condemn thee. Go and sin no more." While reading this story, a thrill of hope floods through us for we perceive that our God is a *forgiving God.*

Of all God's traits exhibited in the life of Jesus, perhaps none are displayed more vividly than the one portrayed on the cross. There the sinless one willingly died for our sins, offering us the gift of eternal life. Is it not evident that *our God loves us*?

Praise God we don't have to worship some unknown deity. Neither must we rely upon our own imagination to construct a god. We have revealed for us the perfect picture of God's nature as it is unfolded in the life of Jesus.

THE WITNESSES OF THIS TRUTH

This was quite a claim for Jesus to make. It was immense in its scope. Certainly there must be something to back up this claim.

That night in the Upper Room, Jesus spoke of two things issuing directly from the Father that attested to who he was. They were his *words* and his *works*. His words, which caused some to say "no one every spoke like this man," came from the Father. He then claimed it was the Father who did the marvelous works he performed and encouraged Philip to believe the works.

This assertion that his words and works validate his claim was reminiscent of an earlier, more in-depth discussion of his authority that Jesus had with the Jews. We find it recorded in John 5:31–39, and in it, Jesus presents four witnesses that testified of who he was.

The first witness he brought to the stand was *John the Baptist*.

Jesus said, **"Ye sent unto John, and he bare witness unto the truth"** (verse 33). John was accepted by the population at large as a great prophet. Jesus himself said there was not a greater man born of women than John.

John's testimony was this: he must increase, and I must decrease. When he saw Jesus coming, he publicly proclaimed, **"Behold the Lamb of God, which taketh away the sin of the world. This is he of whom I said, After me cometh a man which is preferred before me: for he was before me"** (John 1:29–30). So the greatest of men gave testimony of who Jesus was.

The next witness to testify was *the works Jesus did*.

After presenting the greatest of men, Jesus asserted, **"But I have greater witness than that of John: for the works which the Father**

hath given me to finish, the same works that I do, bear witness of me, that the Father hath sent me" (verse 36).

Every step Jesus walked, every sermon he preached, and every miracle he performed spoke loud and clear of who he was. There was no false step in his walk. He preached God's Kingdom, love, and forgiveness. No miracle he did was self-serving but was for good.

Have you ever wondered why since Jesus did not seek to promote himself, he did so many miracles? I believe there are at least three reasons why he performed miracles.

To begin with, he did them for the sake of those he healed. He was so moved with compassion that he sought to relieve the individual's suffering. On top of that, however, each miracle illustrated some spiritual truth. The raising of Lazarus from the dead, for example, illustrated that Jesus was the resurrection and the life. Lastly, each miracle was a sign to Israel to validate the words he spoke and testify that he was the Son of God. Every move Jesus made cried out "I am he who was from everlasting to everlasting. I AM."

Next up to the witness stand was *the Father himself.*

It must have really shaken his listeners to attention when Jesus claimed, **"And the Father himself, which hath sent me, hath borne witness of me"** (verse 37). Talk about a wake-up call. The audacity of that claim had to have made it clear to all those around that Jesus was claiming to be the Messiah, sent from God.

There were at least three occasions where the Father spoke publicly to affirm that this was his Son.

The first occasion was at the baptism of Jesus and was in response to his obedience to the Father's will. The Father sent the Spirit upon him, affirmed his sonship, and said, "I am well pleased with him."

We next hear the Father speak on the Mount of Transfiguration. With Peter, James, and John looking on, Jesus is transformed to his glorified state and carries on a conversation with Moses and Elijah. Peter, overwhelmed by this spectacular scene, rashly suggests they build three booths for worship: one for Moses, one for Elijah, and one for Jesus. Intending to correct Peter's view, the Father singles out Jesus and says, "*This one* is my beloved Son. Hear ye him!"

The third time the Father spoke was strictly to give testimony to all those around. It happened in Jerusalem during the last week of Jesus's life. It is recorded in John 12:28–30. Jesus prayed: **"Father, glorify thy name. Then came there a voice from heaven, saying, I have both glorified it, and will glorify it again. The people therefore, that stood by, and heard it, said that it thundered: others said, an angel spake to him. Jesus answered and said, This voice came not because of me, but for your sakes."**

We have seen an impressive array of witnesses approach the stand. We have heard from the greatest of men, we have seen the works that Jesus did, and we have heard the Father speak. But there is one more witness to be heard. The last witness Jesus presented was *the scriptures*.

Jesus points to that which was very precious to the hearts of the Jewish rabbis. He challenged: **"Search the scriptures; for in them ye think ye have eternal life: and they are they which testify of me"** (verse 39).

Jesus told them the very scriptures they venerated, the scriptures that had been entrusted to them by God, gave testimony of who Christ was. No one else could have ever met the criteria of scripture. No one but Jesus. He alone fit the prophesies.

The witness is overwhelming. With assurance, we can say Jesus is the only begotten Son of God and the incarnation of God in the flesh.

Do you want to know what God is like? Look at Jesus.

Do you want to be able to have fellowship with your Creator? Go through Jesus Christ.

Do you want a faith that will bring comfort during the time of trial? Do you want something that is genuine and real? Throw away your preconceived notions. Don't try to shape God into what you think he should be. With an open heart, seek to know him.

Behold the Lamb of God who takes away the sins of the world.

Look to Jesus.

* * * * *

Let's go back into our imagination to Elnathan.

It is a quiet night out in the field as you and three other shepherds sit together watching your sheep. You have found a rock overhang. From its mouth, you can sit and keep an eye on the flock. This vantage point gives you a good view of the entire field. You can see any predator coming. You can also see Bethlehem off to the side.

It is a calm and slightly brisk night. The sky is unusually clear. It might have been nights like this when the shepherd boy David would gaze into the expanse of stars and write his beautiful psalms. The vista of sky, field, and town would certainly lend itself to the poetic nature, but Elnathan could not enjoy it.

So much has happened in the last few weeks since the loss of your child. You are past the grieving stage, but do you really ever get past it? All sorts of questions have been flooding your mind, and they have left you feeling empty inside. While you are working your way through your grief, you have begun to question your beliefs. You have been hard-pressed to find any comfort.

Yes, you have been disillusioned by the temple system, but you have always believed in God. You now wonder about God.

"If only I knew God understood and cared for me, I could handle all of this," you are thinking.

Your attention is suddenly drawn to the conversation the other shepherds are having. For the first time, you notice an unusually bright star. Something is out of place here. From your childhood, you have gazed up at the stars, and you know each star by name. This star you do not recognize. It just shouldn't be there. As the night begins to brighten slightly, someone comments that it must be some sort of sign. Certainly, something monumental must be about to happen.

Suddenly, the sky seems to explode with light. It seems to you that the whole earth is caressed with these brilliant rays.

The only word to describe your feelings at this moment is FEAR! Elnathan found himself shivering, face down on the ground. He vaguely thought he remembered one of his friends saying something along the lines of the "end of the world." At the moment, you are not inclined to argue with him.

Then you hear the words "Fear not." Looking up, you see a most amazing sight. An indescribable being is standing before you. Certainly a being like this must be the angel of the Lord. His words produce calm within your very being.

"Fear not: for, behold, I bring you good tidings of great joy, which shall be to all people. For unto you is born this day in the city of David a Savior, which is Christ the Lord. And this shall be a sign unto you; ye shall find the babe wrapped in swaddling clothes, lying in a manger" (Luke 2:10–12).

As you gaze in wonder at this sight, the sky is suddenly filled from horizon to horizon with these messengers. The sound that begins to swell around you is the sound of praise. You can't really describe it. You don't know if it is singing or shouting, but it is the most beautiful and lyrical thing you have ever heard. The sound seems to start up in the heavens and roll in waves down the earth. There it engulfs you and seems to lift you up with it as it rolls back into Heaven. Over and over it swells. Wave after wave of praise continues to sweep over you.

"Glory to God in the highest and on earth peace, good will towards men" (Luke 2:14).

Just as suddenly as they came, they are gone, leaving the stillness of the night as they found it. But you realize it isn't quiet. You still hear praise. Your friends are lifting their hands, praising God. You realize it is your own voice that is also joined in praise. "Glory and praise to God who has shown us his great mercy!"

As what has happened begins to sink in, Josiah, one of your friends says, "We must find the child. Certainly he must be the one foretold; the Messiah. Quickly, we must be going!"

All thoughts of the sheep are now gone as you rush toward the town of Bethlehem. Approaching the village, you are met by people coming out of town. They are asking excitedly, "What is all the commotion about? We thought we saw a bright light in the field. We heard a noise, but we could not distinguish it."

Josiah stops and begins to relate to them the message from the angels. He has gathered quite a crowd listening to his every word, but you press on. You must find this child!

As you search in all the normal places, several things are running through your mind. The question you asked yourself just prior to the angels appearing keeps popping up in your thoughts, "If I could only know that God cares . . . If I could only know that God cares . . . Can I know the mind of God? Does he understand me?"

Each time you bring to mind that question, the angel's message resounds in your head. "Unto you is born this day . . . Unto you is born . . . *Unto you*!" It's as if something deep inside has personalized it. "Elnathan, unto you!"

Finally, you are directed to a stable. As you enter, you see an average-looking couple, nothing extraordinary about them. She is exhausted and resting from the ordeal of birth, but there is still a glow of joy on her face. Your request is simple, "May we see the child?"

You are brought over to where the mother is. There in a crudely improvised feeding trough, your eyes fall upon a vision of peace and tranquility. The baby is resting. His eyes are slightly closed. A lamb standing beside the manger sticks his head over the side and licks the hand of the infant just before it is lead away.

Ever so slightly, the infant opens his eyes. Maybe it's your imagination, but you feel like he's looking right at you. Deep inside, warmth you can't explain takes the place of that cold emptiness that had resided there. It courses through your body till it reaches your eyes. You are really amazed to find tears running down your face.

For the first time in your life, you feel like God cares for you.

What you are gazing upon is God's gift to you.

You are literally seeing the expression of God's heart.

"God has not forgotten us," you are thinking. "He has fulfilled his promise."

There's a new hope swelling up within you for you have seen him, "God with us."

> **"That which was from the beginning, which we have heard, which we have seen with our eyes, which we have looked upon, and our hands have handled, of the Word of life"**
>
> —First John 1:1

The Scripture

OVERCOMING POWERLESSNESS

"Verily, verily, I say unto you, he that believeth on me, the works that I do shall he do also; and greater works than these shall he do, because I go unto my Father.

And whatever ye shall ask in my name, that will I do, that the Father may be glorified in the Son.

If ye shall ask anything in my name, I will do it.

If ye love me, keep my commandments."

—John 14:12–15

Chapter 8

OVERCOMING POWERLESSNESS

The electronic bolt clicked shut with a loud metallic strike. The acoustics of the high-ceilinged jail pod (cell) gave it a slightly hollow echo, accentuating the ominous feeling of being locked in. I was on my own now.

For about a year, I had been helping with the Solid Rock Jail and Prison Ministry. Under the direction of Jim Mantooth and Lynn Phillips, this ministry has prospered with the blessing of God. One of their outreaches is in the Cherokee County Jail. Every Thursday night, they would go into the jail and hold service in four different pods. They would be taken through a series of locked doors and left with the inmates who wanted to have a service. You were basically locked in with them.

About once every six weeks, when one of the regulars would be out, I would be called upon to go in and preach the Word to them.

The first time I went in, I was excited about trying something new, but I was a little unsure of how I would be received by the inmates. As the service started, a friend of mine began singing an old gospel song, "When He Reached Down His Hand for Me." There was just something about that song being sung in that setting that got "all over" me. As I listened, I began looking around at all the inmates.

Something really began to stir inside of me. These were men who desperately needed to hear the life-changing gospel. When I got up to preach, it could have been Sunday morning in a country Baptist church. God moved in a marvelous way, and three souls were saved.

From that time on, I looked forward to every opportunity I received to go in, and I always felt comfortable there. The men always seemed to be receptive to the gospel, and we saw many people saved. But this Thursday night was different. There had been some trouble.

Before we arrived, one troublemaker had influenced several of the other men, and together, they stood up and said, "Those preachers aren't coming down here tonight." They intimidated those who wanted to have the services and basically challenged the guards.

The guards weren't about to let their authority be challenged. Besides which, they were always very appreciative and supportive of our efforts. They did a partial "lockdown." The ringleader and a few others were isolated in solitary.

Of course, the pod it had happened in was the pod I was scheduled to be in that night. I usually always went in with a singer who would lead some songs and then sing a special. Of all the times it could have happened, this was the week we couldn't find a singer to go in with me. I was going in all by myself.

The guards had warned us ahead of time what had happened, so I was a little apprehensive as I passed through the security doors. For the first time since I had been coming to the jail, I did not want to be there.

As the guards led me into pod D, there was an unmistakable air of resentment drifting over the room. The hard looks they were directing toward me didn't exactly settle my stomach down. It was tied in one huge knot. Hanging over the entire room, I knew beyond the shadow of a doubt was an evil spirit.

After opening in prayer I said, "Let's start by singing a song together." I chose a song that in the past they had enjoyed and really sang out on and began to lead them in song.

I was singing solo.

No one else was singing. *No one* participated. They just sat there, glaring at me with a look of hatred that said, "We don't want you here, and you're not going to be able to do anything tonight."

You have to understand a few things about my nature to truly understand what I had going against me in this situation.

To begin with, I had been saved at an early age, was raised in a Christian home, and had been spared much of the troubles that these men faced. The entire environment of jail, associating with an element that broke the law, was foreign to my nature. By God's grace, I had never walked in their shoes and had never been in trouble a day in my life.

Add to that the fact that, basically, I have a reserved nature. When you're young, they call it "being shy." When you're an adult, they call it a reserved nature. By my very nature, I would have been an unlikely candidate to be a preacher.

So there I was. A shy young preacher unaccustomed to this environment locked in jail all alone with a bunch of inmates who didn't want me there. The prospect of something happening to me was a very real possibility.

As I was reading my scripture, a very familiar urging went through me. God began to take control of that service, and my uneasiness was replaced with an amazing boldness. I changed my sermon in midstream and preached a strong salvation message from the Book of Romans.

Regardless of the response of the inmates, it was Sunday morning church for the preacher all over again. When I think back on some of the statements I made, it's clear to me they were prompted by the Holy Spirit. I would never have made statements that bold in that situation. In dealing with the fact that we are all sinners, I said, "The reason some people don't want preachers to come down here is that they are sinners, they revel in their sin, and they don't want their wickedness exposed." I can't believe I said that!

Then I began to tell them of God's provision for our salvation—how God sent his Son to die for our sins and offer us the gift of eternal life. As I did, something began to happen in the hard hearts of those men. They began to soften. Some who had gone back to their cots began to drift over and join the service. The looks of hatred began to abate, being replaced with eyes that were misty with tears. It was something I could not have accomplished with all of my powers of persuasion. It was clear God was doing a work.

Many services there had gotten better responses. No one responded in this service. WE had seen many people saved on other Thursday nights, but this is the one that sticks out in my mind. It was memorable for two reasons. First, for the amazing boldness he gave a shy preacher, and second, for the supernatural softening of the hearts of hardened men. I have seen God work in many circumstances, but this time was especially meaningful to me because of the adverse circumstances.

What was it that transformed a preacher and softened hearts? Before we went down, all of us who were going to minister had joined hands in a circle and prayed, "Father, in the name of Jesus, fill your servants with the Holy Spirit. *We are totally dependent upon you.*"

* * * * *

Nothing can be more frustrating and discouraging to a child of God than to feel like he is not accomplishing anything.

In some cases, it is all in a person's imagination. However, it is sad but true that many Christians will live their entire lives without making the slightest impact on their world. This is because their lives are lived totally for themselves. Their trademark has become their selfishness, and everything they do is for their number one: self.

This is not the person I really want to deal with in this chapter, however. The person I just described needs desperately to come face to face with Jesus Christ and catch a glimpse of themselves as God sees them. Only then can they begin to grow to be salt and light to the world, but that will be covered in another chapter.

The person I really want to look at here is the person who loves the Lord Jesus and is earnestly trying to serve him but feels he is not accomplishing anything. It seems like he is *powerless* in all he tries.

All that this man tries, whether in ministry or at his secular job, has no measurable results. He feels like a failure and often quits.

Without something to strive for, his life seems empty and void, and he is brought to the point of personal crisis.

This is not the pattern God intended for his children. In the quiet of the Upper Room, Jesus made a promise to his disciples. On the surface, it is a promise that might be hard to comprehend, but it is glorious. It is, however, a promise that is contingent upon certain things.

Let's take a close look at this promise and the prerequisites to successfully claim it.

THE PROMISE OF GREATER WORKS

To fully understand the promise, you cannot just pull verse 12 out and look at it alone. You have to follow the conversation that was taking place. It began with Philip's request to see the Father.

Jesus responded, "Have I been with you all this time, and yet you still don't recognize me? If you have seen me, you have seen the father."

Jesus then pointed to his words and his works as witnesses to who he was. He affirmed that indeed it was the Father who was doing the works he did.

As we stated in the last chapter, these works were the many miracles Jesus performed while he was in the world. They were performed in order to give testimony to the veracity of Jesus's words. Those works spoke of his character, power, and deity. They were designed to aid weak faith.

He went on to say, "If you are finding it difficult to believe my words, then believe the works I am doing for they witness of me. Believe the works!"

Then Jesus made this most astounding promise: **"He that believeth on me, the works that I do shall he do also; and greater works than these shall he do; because I go unto my Father."**

Jesus had not yet done his greatest work; he had not gone to the cross yet. That was a work we could never top or even duplicate. We could never die for the sins of the world.

What Jesus was telling his disciples, however, was they would perform greater works than those "sign works" he did while he walked the earth. That brings up a confusing question. In what way could the works the disciples performed be considered greater than the miracles Jesus performed?

The work the disciples would do, or rather that the Holy Spirit would do through the disciples, was the great harvest of souls gathered together in the first century. The harvest would begin on the day of Pentecost and continue on past the times of the apostles. It continues today with the proclamation of the gospel.

Their works were not greater in scope or degree but in the type of works that they were and in their long-range effect. The physical healings Jesus performed were temporary in nature. The blind eyes made to see were eventually closed in death. The lame feet made to walk were soon laid to rest. Even Lazarus, who was raised from the dead, entered death again. The physical administrations of Jesus's power were strictly temporary, and as we have mentioned before, they were given as signs to testify of him.

The souls that were born again by the Spirit of God had eternal impact. *Those souls live on eternally* and are in the presence of Jesus. When the apostles preached the gospel with thousands being converted, they were reaping eternal dividends.

In the same vein, whenever we are involved in the proclamation of the gospel, we are likewise investing in souls, making an impact on eternity. It is to the person who through preaching, singing, teaching, or witnessing seeks to spread the good news that this promise is given. Whenever we promote Jesus, it is then that we accomplish the most eternal good.

Before we go on, let me make two statements about the promise. It is in *doing his work* that the promise is made. It cannot be claimed for selfish reasons or gain.

Also, the promise of greater works is *the promise of power beyond ourselves*. There is no room for boasting by the disciples or by anyone else for the power is from the Lord.

Why is it, then, that we often see powerlessness in some people's service to the Lord? Why do some efforts seem vain and empty? Why do we often see a weak or dead church?

WHAT CAUSES POWERLESSNESS?

Most of the time, powerlessness in our service will stem from one of three things.

Timidity will defeat you before you even get started. If you are plagued by timidity, you might never date to enact bold measures for the glory of the Lord. There is that ever present fear of failure that will stop you cold. Often we don't accomplish anything because WE NEVER ATTEMPT ANYTHING.

How many times have you been impressed to share the gospel with someone, but some deep hidden fear prevailed and you let that opportunity pass by? That is timidity defeating your service.

If we are going to accomplish anything, timidity must be conquered. We must have a supernatural boldness beyond our efforts.

There are times, though, when we put forth a genuine effort and find we are stopped cold by *inability*. We might find that we have insufficient knowledge, experience, or wisdom to finish what we have started. Nothing is more frustrating than to find yourself in the middle of something and not knowing what to do next.

Sometimes we put our very BEST efforts into service, and it turns out to be not nearly good enough. We must know what our limitations are and understand that without the Lord, we ARE NOT able to effectively serve him.

I firmly believe, however, that by far, the most common cause of powerlessness is *independence*. We try to serve the Lord, but we do it independently of the Lord. We jump into something without seeking his direction because it seems like a good opportunity. We try to use our own ingenuity to do the work. We rely upon our personalities, talents, or program to fight spiritual warfare, and all these are sadly lacking.

You cannot substitute personality for the power of God. Entertainment will not do the work of the Holy Spirit. My talents could never CHANGE A LIFE.

To change lives, to make an impact on eternity, I must have the miraculous working of God on my ministry. I cannot work independently of him in the energy of the flesh. I must be TOTALLY DEPENDENT upon him. I might be able to work up some surface results using my talents and ingenuity, but I do not have the power to change a human heart. It has to be someone greater than I who does the work.

In the verses following the promise of greater works, we will find the key to claiming his power.

DEALING WITH POWERLESSNESS

If you have been struggling with powerlessness and you desire the hand of God upon your service, the first thing you must do is really kind of basic. Before anything else, you must *acknowledge your dependence upon the Lord*. You must understand you CANNOT DO IT without his touch.

Right at the beginning, you have to deal with that independent streak that wants to be in control of everything. This necessitates my giving up control and yielding to the Holy Spirit's control.

Let me be quick to add that saying the words is a lot easier than actually doing it. Sometimes, I confess, I feel like I don't know how to yield control to him. But it must begin with the realization of my helplessness and my desire to give up my hand of control in the best way I know how.

After you have recognized the fact that you are totally dependent upon him, you must then *ask the Father in the name of Jesus* for the strength and the power necessary to handle your particular task.

Directly after he spoke about greater works, Jesus said, **"And whatsoever ye shall ask in my name, that will I do."** That this promise is not a "Santa Claus" provision (a reason to ask for anything selfishly) is evident through its context. It is specifically tied to the previous promise of greater works (doing HIS work) and two items that follow. It was never intended for us to claim this verse in order to lavish all sorts of luxuries upon ourselves, but we CAN ask for his hand upon our service to him.

When he said we were to ask in his name, it means more than just tacking "in Jesus's name" onto the end of our prayers. It is recognition of his lordship and our submission to him. We identify our request with that most holy name and present it to the Father.

The association of the prayer with the name of the Son catches the Father's attention, and if the following items tied to it are in line, it moves the Father to action. He looks at his child in prayer and says, "He is one of mine, and he is praying in the name of my son. I will answer."

Let me add right here that it is a petition we make of the Lord. We never demand or "command" God, as some false prophets would have you believe. He is a holy God. I am a frail human being. He is my heavenly Father. I am his child. I would no more challenge his holiness than I would dishonor my earthly father by trying to command him.

In the very same breath that he promises answered prayer, Jesus states what should be our motive in prayer and, in fact, what should be the motive for our service. Our motive should be to *glorify God by lifting up Jesus.* He said he would answer our petitions made in the name of Jesus **that the Father may be glorified in the Son**.

Ask yourself these questions: will the things I am praying for glorify God, or does it merely satisfy my own desires? What is my motive for doing what I do?

We should be driven by an all-consuming love for Jesus. If we are his disciple, our desire should be that every step we take would bring glory to God. If we love him, our every little action should speak of Jesus. Our speech should be seasoned with those things that are pure and holy, giving testimony of the saving grace of our Lord.

It is sad to have to admit it, but many who seek a position in God's work do so because they desire the eminence it brings. They strive to advance themselves.

Do you want POSITION, or do you want POWER? If it is position you want, you can find it by your own ingenuity, but your reward will be limited to the world. You will not make a lasting impression for the kingdom of God. If it is God's power that you want, deny yourself, ask for his hand upon your life, and seek to glorify him with everything you do. It is then that you can impact eternity.

There is one other thing Jesus ties to this promise, and it absolutely will effect what kind of power you have. Jesus demands *obedience*.

It was not a coincident that in this context Jesus said, **"If you love me, keep my commandments."** Obedience is essential to answered prayer and the power of God.

Obedience can affect the outcome of our prayers in two ways. First, it suggests the Lord is guiding us, and we are obedient to do what he says. We go where he says go. We do what he says do. If for some reason we fail to follow his leading and go our own way, it is disobedience. God is not obligated to answer our every whim then.

Second, certain moral imperatives are spelled out in God's Word. God requires a clean vessel to work in. If someone falls into immorality and does not repent of it, God will not acknowledge his prayer. To live in immorality is willful disobedience.

No doubt someone is reading this right now and is discouraged because all their efforts have produced no visible results. Don't make the mistake of trying to measure your effectiveness or worth by whether or not you see tangible results. You may not see all that God is doing through you. If you must measure success, measure it by obedience. If God has directed you and you have been obedient to his command, you have been successful, and perhaps only Heaven will reveal what has actually been accomplished through your life.

Let me reiterate something I have already indicated. Seeking to glorify God and obedience to him are so closely connected in this passage with asking in prayer that they cannot be separated without doing great harm to the meaning of that scripture. Jesus's intention was to show his disciples the connection between them.

This is the way Jesus laid it out for his disciples: "I promise that you will do greater works, but in order to do them you must let me work through you. If you want that power, then acknowledge your dependence on me, ask for it in the name of Jesus, seek to glorify God, and be obedient to my every command. Then you shall have power."

Have you ever felt timid or afraid to share your faith? His touch can give you the boldness you need.

Do you feel as if you are inadequate to serve him and you just do not have the ability to do some things? Let me assure you that you really don't have the ability, but he enables us and develops those abilities within use as we grow in him.

Have you tried to serve him in your own strength and failed? Don't try to do a work for him, but let *him* do the work through you.

Every one of the causes of powerlessness can be overcome. As we will see in the next chapter, the agent he uses to give us power is the Holy Spirit. As we yield to him and ask in prayer, he gives us the power we need. We then have the privilege to participate in the great work of God, his continuing work through us, the claiming of souls for eternity.

The Scripture

THE COMING OF THE COMFORTER

"If ye love me, keep my commandments. And I will pray the Father, and he shall give you another Comforter, that he may abide with you forever; Even the Spirit of truth, whom the world cannot receive, because it seeth him not, neither knoweth him: but ye know him; for he dwelleth with you, and shall be in you. I will not leave you comfortless, I will come to you."

—John 14:15–18

"But the Comforter, who is the Holy Ghost, whom the Father will send you in my name, he shall teach you all things, and bring all things to your remembrance, whatsoever I have said unto you."

—John 14:26

"But when the Comforter is come, whom I will send unto you from the Father, even the Spirit of truth, who proceedeth from the Father, he shall testify of me; and ye also shall bear witness, because ye have been with me from the beginning."

—John 15:26–27

"Nevertheless, I tell you the truth: It is expedient for you that I go away; for if I do not go away, the Comforter will not come unto you; but if I depart, I will send him unto you.

And when he is come, he shall reprove the world of sin, and of righteousness, and of judgment: of sin, because they believed not on me; of righteousness, because I go to my Father, and ye see me no more; of judgment, because the prince of this world is judged.

I have yet many things to say unto you, but ye cannot hear them now.

Howbeit, when he, the Spirit of truth, is come, he will guide you into all truth; for he shall not speak of himself, but whatever he shall hear, that shall he speak; and he will show you things to come. He shall glorify me; for he shall receive of mine, and shall show it unto you. All things that the Father hath are mind; therefore said I, that he shall take of mine, and shall show it unto you."

—John 16:7–15

Chapter 9

THE COMING OF THE COMFORTER

Beau was the perfect example of one who had learned of his shortcomings the hard way, by experience.

Beau was the thoroughbred French poodle who thought he ruled the Foster domain during my formative years. He had no comprehension of the fact that "bigger" dogs could do bodily harm to him. When he was very young, he had a keen sense that our yard was his "turf." If a squirrel, cat, or another dog trespassed on his turf, he would take off in an explosion of energy and proceed to chase them off his domain. Amazingly, enough he got away with it for a number of years.

One day, he came to a rude awakening. He ran up against a much bigger dog. We didn't see the encounter, but it must have been vicious. He came home whimpering with blood right below his neck where a dog had latched on to him, picked him up, and shook him around. It left a lasting impression on Beau's mind.

It was pretty evident to us which dog did it because from that day forward, Beau lived in fear of the neighborhood German shepherd. If he was out in the yard minding his own business and just happened to see that dog way up the street, he would immediately turn around and trot back to the house, whining to be let in. In short, the dog terrorized him and enjoyed doing it.

There came a day, however, when that big bully of a dog over-played his hand.

I was standing just inside the door to our house that day, just scanning the neighborhood as I enjoyed a beautiful, sunny day. Beau was out in the yard taking care of his normal business. Unseen by Beau, his adversary had sneaked up on him. I saw him hiding behind my car. He had his head down and was silently creeping around the front of the car. His eyes were fastened on Beau, oblivious to any-thing else around him. He looked like a panther stalking his prey.

At the last instant, Beau turned and saw him. I had no idea he could move so quickly. He turned and began running toward the house as fast as he could with his antagonist right on his tail. With every step, he was yelping as though that dog already had a hold on him. With the fear and terror in his voice, you would have thought it was the devil himself that was on his tail.

Now you've got to understand I did not exactly appreciate that big dog picking on my little dog. I jumped out the door and started yelling at him, "Hey! Get outa here! Go on, get!" When the dog saw me, he stopped dead in his tracks.

When Beau saw me, the most amazing transformation came over my little dog. He stopped and spun around to face that big bully. He was no longer running though he was face to face with a dog twice his size. His teeth were bared. He wasn't yelping now. He was *growling*!

You've never seen such a brave little fellow! As the shepherd turned to run off, Beau gave chase. It was really kind of a funny sight watching that tiny dog chase that huge dog. The whole time he was chasing him, he kept glancing back over his shoulder to make sure I was coming with him.

He chased the doge off our property, and as the dog ran up the street, Beau stood on the edge of our yard barking after him as if to say "And if you come back, you'll be more of the same!"

It's amazing what seeing your master and sensing his presence alongside you can do for your bravery.

* * * * *

The one who gives us the power to serve the Lord effectively is the Holy Spirit.

The one who gives us the boldness to face overwhelming opposition is God's Holy Spirit.

He is the one who gives us the strength to stand when we are dead tired.

It is the Holy Spirit that speaks a word of comfort to the heart that has been broken. He is the one who makes the presence of Jesus so very precious as we read our Bible, think upon God's goodness, or lift up a prayer to the Father. In fact, he is the one who takes our prayer to the Father in the name of the Son. His work is indispensable to our living the Christian life. We just can't do it without him.

His coming was prophesied in Old Testament scriptures such as Joel 2:28–29: **"And it shall come to pass afterward, that I will pour out my Spirit upon all flesh; and your sons and your daughters shall prophesy, your old men shall dream dreams, your young men shall see visions; And, also, upon the servant and upon the handmaids in those days will I pour out my Spirit."**

What was prophesied in the scripture was promised by the Savior. Jesus, in the Upper Room, was attempting to do two things with the words he was speaking. He was *preparing* his disciples for his departure, and he was *promising* the coming of the Holy Spirit.

What was about to transpire was incomprehensible to the disciples. Jesus was leaving them. They would no longer have his physical presence with them. They had invested three years of their lives following Jesus, and now they were on the verge of losing him. It turned out devastating enough as it was, but without preparation, it probably would have been more than they could bear.

There's no question that the talk of Jesus being put to death, of his leaving, was highly disturbing to the disciples. But even though the words were difficult, they were spoken through the Savior's mercy. Without the preparation, the shock of his death might have been too much for them. The Lord's mercy was endeavoring to soften the blow and prepare them for the worst.

At times, the Lord tells us things we do not want to hear. He may use the scripture to show us where we fall short, or he may use a friend giving godly counsel. Hearing what we don't want to hear can sometimes be a blessing in disguise. The Lord's compassion may be at work in those words. They may come as a warning or merely to prepare us for a storm we are about to enter. But it is always his mercy at work in the lives of his children.

In retrospect, the disciples had no cause to be so disturbed by his words. What was unfolding was in accordance to God's plan. What seemed to them as a great loss would turn out to be a cause for rejoicing. It would be through his death that their sins would be washed away. In just a few days, there would be the joy of seeing the resurrected Lord, but for now, all they could see was Jesus was leaving them. *They had a limited view.*

While we are in this flesh, we are hampered by a limited view. We cannot see behind the scenes. What may seem devastating to us might be of great benefit, and only the passing of time or the glory of eternity will reveal it to us.

Jesus tried to prepare them for the unthinkable, and because of their limited view, he left them a promise. His promise was the Father would send a "comforter"—the Holy Spirit.

THE ONE HE WAS SENDING

When Jesus called the Spirit a *comforter*, it was a term descriptive of what his relationship to believers would be.

The term *comforter* literally means "*one who is called alongside to give aid.*" He is to believers the one who walks by their side, assuring them of God's presence and being a constant helper and companion.

When he said he was sending "another" comforter, it was indicative of the truth that the disciples at that time already had a comforter in the person of Jesus. It was a function Jesus was already fulfilling in their lives. But Jesus was leaving, so he was sending the Spirit to fill that void. They would no longer enjoy the physical presence of Jesus. They would not have him to walk alongside of them, but instead they would experience his presence through the person of the Holy Spirit. In that sense, Jesus could say, **"I will come to you."**

As believers in this century, we have never looked upon the physical form of the Lord Jesus. We have not had the privilege of hearing words spoken directly from the lips of the one born in Bethlehem. But we have known his loving presence by the Holy Spirit dwelling within us and walking beside us.

It is him, the third person of the Godhead, who acts as a comforter and our helper in all things.

As our *guide*, he directs our steps as we yield to his leadership. Have you ever been in a tough situation and you had no idea what the solution was? Did you go to God in prayer, take down your Bible, pour through its pages, and wonder, "What in the world am I going to do?" Then, in your time of communing with God, did a course of action become clear to you? That was our companion guiding our feet.

As we grow in grace, he is our *teacher*, illuminating the scriptures for us. First, he testifies to the reliability of the scripture. Then as the Christian delves into the word, he takes that word, implants it within the child of God, instructs from it, and nourishes that word until it begins to shape and change our lives. He teaches us how we ought to live.

When we are experiencing heartbreak, the Comforter becomes our *encourager*. There are times when our human friends cannot help; they have no words to say. Sometimes they may fail to be there when you need them the most, making the pain you are going through seem that much more intense. It is then that you feel loving arms wrapped around you and hear the Lord say "I love you. I will be with you always."

How can he be always with us? He is with us through the person of the Spirit—our constant companion walking alongside us. Who else could bring comfort like him?

His work within us is essential to living the Christian life.

LIFE WITHOUT THE COMFORTER?

We so take his work within us for granted that to fully appreciate just how necessary he is, ask yourself this question: What would life be like without the Comforter?

When Jesus said **"I will not leave you comfortless,"** he was literally saying "I will not leave you as orphans." That word amply describes what life without him would be like. We would be without a guiding hand; children without a father. Orphans.

Can you imagine that when you need a friend, you would find no one there? Maybe your earthly friends have failed you, and you are facing a test all alone. You need a hand holding yours. You need someone to say "I am with you." You turn to all sides. There is no word of encouragement. You are alone. You are orphaned.

What happens when doubts about your salvation arise? You try to read your Bible, but it seems like gibberish to you. You cannot understand it. There is no one to guide you to understanding. You look for a touch of assurance, and there is none.

A life-changing decision confronts you, and you have limited information to go on. You are on your own. There is no divine guidance. There are all sorts of traps laid for you, which you cannot see. How do you order your steps?

Temptation to do evil presents itself. It strikes in an area you are weak in. There is no restraining hand. How can you stay pure?

Then the unthinkable happens—the one you love the most passes away. You are alone in your grief. There is no comforting hand. How do you cope?

Life for the Christian without the Comforter would be empty, barren, and miserable. You would be alone—orphaned.

Do you see how vital he is to us? Thank God, Jesus sent us a Comforter **"that he may abide with us forever."** We could know his touch and receive his comfort because, as Jesus said, **"He dwelleth with you, and shall be in you."**

HIS PURPOSE FOR COMING

In examining what the Spirit's purpose is in coming unto believers, there are several things one might state. As we have said, he has come to walk alongside believers and be our helper. Someone might say he has come to empower believers. Certainly it would be correct to call him our teacher—the one who instructs us in godliness.

But all these things could be considered secondary purposes and brought under the umbrella of one all-encompassing purpose. His main purpose in coming into the world is *to glorify Christ.*

Jesus phrased it like this: **"Howbeit when he the Spirit of truth is come . . . he shall not speak of himself . . . . He shall glorify me"** (John 16:13–14). His reason for coming is to lift up and promote the Lord Jesus.

Let me point out also that his purpose is not to emphasize the Holy Spirit; he does not speak of himself. Whenever the Spirit moves, *Jesus* is lifted up. Jesus receives the glory. When the Holy Spirit is on a church or an individual, it will not be the Spirit that is lifted up. All they will want to talk about is Jesus, Jesus, and more Jesus.

One of the ways he will glorify Jesus is in the lives of believers. This is why it is so important that believers live pure lives. This is why they should shine with the joy of the Lord, in spite of circumstances. This is why Christians should never display attitudes that reflect badly on our Lord. The best worker on the job ought to be the child of God. They should reflect godliness for it is the Spirit that ministers to believers to they can exhibit the fruit of the Spirit.

If a man says he is filled with the Holy Spirit, you should be able to see a little bit of Christ in his daily walk. Sadly, too often, the one who claims loud and long that he is Spirit-filled will exhibit very little Christ-likeness. How can a man be like Christ and be mean spirited? I have heard Christians argue a point before, and it would be something that basically I agreed with them on. But they did it in such a way that it embarrassed me, and I wished they had kept their mouth shut. There was no love in the words they spoke.

If we are going to publicly claim to know Christ, let us back it up by how we live. Let us yield to the Holy Spirit and allow him to shape us. Then Christ will be glorified in our lives.

If the Spirit glorifies Jesus in the lives of believers, how does he speak to the lost world?

THE SPIRIT SPEAKING TO A DYING WORLD

Does the Spirit speak to people who do not know him? If he does, what is it he says to them?

Jesus, as recorded in John 16:8–11, said that the Spirit would speak to the world. There he said, **"And when he is come, he will reprove the world of sin, and of righteousness, and of judgment: Of sin, because they believe not on me; of righteousness, because I go to my Father, and ye see me no more; of judgment, because the prince of this world is judged."**

Jesus said that the Spirit would "reprove" the world. There are several such words that can describe the word *reprove*, such as convict, confute, and refute. They all adequately picture the work of the Spirit.

I would like to emphasize two specific words, however, that portray the reproving work of the Spirit. The first is the word *expose*. The Spirit exposes man as he really is and reveals his needs. He tears away our self-erected images and reveals to us who we are without the Lord.

The second portrayal of the Spirit's work is the word *convince*. It is the Spirit that convinces us that Jesus is Lord. He convinces us of our need for salvation. In effect, he convinces us of God's true nature and our own true nature.

By reproving, he both exposes and convinces. This is what I call the *dis*comforting work of the Comforter. The Spirit exposes man as he really is and convinces him of his need for the Lord Jesus. This is very unsettling to people, which is why some react so strongly and feel offended if you speak of their need for salvation. It is discomforting, but if it is responded to properly it leads to great comfort and joy.

So if the Spirit speaks to the world in reproof, what is it that he actually says? Jesus indicated he would speak specifically to three different areas.

First, he said the Spirit would reprove them *of sin*. The very thing that separates man from God is what the Spirit exposes. The Holy Spirit confronts it head on.

You cannot depend on human conscience. Too many people have a seared conscience. That is why they can callously walk all over someone in order to get ahead. The hardened human heart will do evil without regret.

Then the illuminating Comforter comes in, exposing sin for what it is and convincing us God is right, and we really are sinners.

Jesus singled out one specific sin, and it is the single worst sin a man may commit. The Spirit would reprove them **of sin, because they believed not on me**. Unbelief, failure to trust the Lord Jesus, has to be dealt with before anything else is addressed. To reject Jesus is to reject God's provision for our salvation.

It takes the Spirit to expose our sin *and then* convince us of our need for Jesus.

Let me add also that left on my own, I would never have believed I was a sinner. My sinful human nature would never admit I have been wrong about anything. Your nature is the same. We view everything from the perspective of ME! WE need the Spirit to convince us of our need.

The second thing the Spirit would speak to the world of would be *righteousness*. He would lift up God's standard of righteousness which is found in Christ Jesus.

It is Christ's personal righteousness, which is the standard to measure all human beings by. If you were to compare me to another human, I might turn out to look pretty good, depending upon whom you choose to measure me by. But when you measure me next to perfection, place me next to the Lord Jesus and I do not look near so good.

When a man is trying to justify his actions, he will always pick out someone to compare himself with. Inevitably, it will be someone with glaring faults. He will say, "See, I'm just as good as that person, and he claims to be a Christian." The problem is he is using the wrong standard to measure himself by.

There's just something about being placed alongside the beauty of his righteous life that magnifies just how wicked we are. We all fall so far short of God's standard.

Jesus said the coming Comforter would speak of his righteousness because **"I go to my Father, and ye see me no more."** Jesus's life and walk would be the model, the standard of perfection, but Jesus was leaving. He would no longer be in our physical presence so we could view his life and walk. Therefore, it would be the Spirit that would lift up the standard of righteousness and convince man of the worthiness of Christ.

And, finally, the Spirit would speak to the world of *judgment.* There will be a day of reckoning when God puts everything in order. Wrong would be punished, and right would be vindicated.

Every person individually will be judged upon one criteria: what they have done with this man called Jesus? Have they received him as Lord and Savior, or have they neglected his sacrifice for them?

When speaking of judgment, everyone's thinking runs along this line: "Certainly God will not judge me. Surely God thinks the same way I do." Place yourself, as much as is possible, in God's shoes, and it looks much differently. He has done everything to provide us with eternal life. He provided his own Son as a sacrifice for us. He suffered death to offer us the gift of life. To ignore this provision in light of his suffering, is the greatest possible wickedness.

The proof of coming judgment is the fact that Satan is judged. The Spirit would speak of judgment **because the prince of this world is judged.** For all practical purposes, Satan was defeated on the cross. He has been judged, and his stranglehold has been broken. The only power he has over us is what we allow him to have. There is coming a final reckoning when his rule shall once and for all be put down. This is what the Spirit testifies of.

The foundational teaching concerning the Holy Spirit is found here in the Book of John chapters 14–16. What these chapters contain must be understood before we can really comprehend what the work of the Spirit within our lives is all about.

For further study, I have included in appendix 1 a brief and partial study of what the gift of the Holy Spirit means to the believer.

As a foundation, Jesus basically said three things about the coming of the Comforter.

He would lift up, glorify, and promote Jesus.

To the believer, he would be a companion walking with us to give us aid.

To the world, he would come in convincing power to expose and convince them of their need for a Savior.

Praise God! We have not been left on our own, but Jesus has sent a companion to us to be our helper. Thank You, Lord, for the Comforter.

The Scripture

HOW TO HAVE JOY

"I am the true vine, and my Father is the husbandman. Every branch in me that beareth not fruit he taketh away: and every branch that beareth fruit, he purgeth it, that it may bring forth more fruit.

Now ye are clean through the word which I have spoken unto you. Abide in me, and I in you. As the branch cannot bear fruit of itself, except it abide in the vine; no more can ye, except ye abide in me.

I am the vine, ye are the branches: he that abideth in me, and I in him, the same bringeth forth much fruit: for without me ye can do nothing.

If a man abide not in me, he is cast forth as a branch, and is withered; and men gather them, and cast them into the fire, and they are burned.

If ye abide in me, and my words abide in you, ye shall ask what you will, and it shall be done unto you. Herein is my Father glorified, that ye bear much fruit; so shall ye be my disciples.

As the Father hath loved me, so have I loved you: continue ye in my love. If you keep my commandments, ye shall abide in my love; even as I have kept my Father's commandments, and abide in his love.

These things have I spoken unto you, that my joy might remain in you, and that your joy might be full."

—John 15:1–11

Chapter 10

HOW TO HAVE JOY

"You're always in a good mood. Why do you always seem so happy?"

I had been working at this particular location for about six months. It was definitely a non-Christian environment. The job was a pressure cooker with a lot of dissatisfied folks all around me. I had not really thoughts about trying to act like I was happy; I was just trying to get my job done. So when the secretary asked me that question, without giving it a second thought, I gave her my standard answer.

I said, "If you really want to know, I will tell you. It's the joy of the Lord."

After having answered her (correctly, by the way), I stopped to analyze her question and my answer. The more I thought on it, the more I came to a conclusion. From the typically human standpoint, *there was no reason for me to be happy!*

The previous year, even though it had been difficult, had been one of the most satisfying and productive years of my life. I worked for a company and had been with them for six years. I had been in a related field for fifteen years. I was also a bivocational pastor, pastoring a little country church about fifty miles from where I worked. I would take care of my pastoral duties by driving up two or three nights a week after work and spending most of the weekend there. It was a grueling schedule, but it was very gratifying. I thrived on it.

Then a series of events took place that was totally beyond my control. It was like I was standing back watching it unfold and was powerless to do anything about it.

It began when a member of my flock passed away. As pastor, I could always plan my schedule so it would not conflict with work. The one thing you cannot plan for, however, is death. I had perfect attendance and "on-time" record for several years and had not taken any time off except for scheduled vacations. Others routinely got off on the spur of the moment, so I went in to ask my boss for two hours off in the middle of the day to do the funeral. I offered to come in early, stay late, or whatever was necessary to be able to do it.

The first words out of his mouth were an ultimatum. "You're going to have to choose between your job and your church. *This*," he said, "is your main job."

Taken somewhat aback, I responded, "There's no choice there, and I'm not going to make that choice."

After talking back and forth all day about it, he finally terminated me. I had been placed in a position, and it had been phrased in such a way that the outcome was assured.

Just one month later, I accidentally walk in on a secret deacons' meeting, called without the knowledge of the pastor. They took the opportunity since I had walked in on it to air out their complaints. The disagreement was over doctrine *and* practice. I will be agreeable on a lot of things, but I will not compromise on the scripture.

They finally came around to saying, "We can't have you as our pastor any longer." They went on to say they *would not* bring it before the church.

After praying about it for a week I decided that in order to avoid a split (which the church had already been through far too many of them before I got there), I would resign. I feared the next split would be the death blow to that church, and there were some sweet people there whom I loved dearly. I did not want to put them through that.

Within a period of one month, I had lost my job over the ministry and then lost that particular ministry.

The job I was presently working was a huge cut in annual pay. Along the way, I also had several unexpected surprises: a car accident, a tree blew over on my home, and taxes hit me unusually hard that year, among other things. The savings I had worked so hard for the past seventeen years had dwindled significantly within the space of a few months. Financially, things looked bleak and did not appear like they would get much better.

On top of all that, opportunities for ministry were slow in coming, which can be very frustrating for a preacher.

From a human perspective, there were not many reasons to be happy. As I examined my answer to that secretary, however, I realized there really was a deep-seated joy in my heart. I also came to the conclusion that if this chain of events had happened to me just a couple of years earlier, I would not have been able to handle it all. God had somehow done a miraculous work in my heart.

However, I have to be perfectly honest about something. Regardless of what that secretary said, I was *not* always in a good mood. There were times I came to work in a terrible mood, and I'm ashamed to say I did not reflect much of Christ in me. I had some very difficult days.

Yet there was no escaping the fact that there was a joy deep down inside me that was supernatural. Yes, I could tell that secretary it was the joy of the Lord. It was not mere words.

I had spent time with Jesus that morning, and there was joy.

* * * * *

When Thomas Jefferson penned the Declaration of Independence, he spoke of certain inalienable rights, which included life, liberty, and the "pursuit of happiness." It seems like ever since then, Americans, so given to extremes, have given themselves to pursuing this elusive dream called happiness. In our present decade, we have become an entertainment-crazed society. All of our leisure time is seemingly geared toward our pleasure.

Relaxation and leisure, frankly, are necessary for our mental and emotional well-being. I enjoy it as well. Have you noticed, however, there is precious little long-term "happiness" affixed to it? There certainly is no deep-seated "joy" in the hearts of the majority of people.

The problem lies in how people set out to find happiness. They base their pursuit of happiness on one of two things. They will either base it on *gratifying self,* or they will long for *acceptance by another person.* What they may not realize is these means are destructive to the end they are trying to achieve. THEIR OWN CHOICES are disruptive to their pursuit.

Take, for instance, the man who is given to self-gratification. He is geared to indulging in personal pleasure. In his search, he collects all sorts of "things." You may have seen his motto on a T-shirt: "In the end, the one with the most toys WINS."

His gratifying of self will, in the short-term, bring pleasure but will not produce lasting joy. The happiness found in it is illusionary. The selfishness inherent in this approach will, before long, alienate those around him, and he may find himself very much alone. He has not been fulfilled by self-gratification, and his own efforts have destroyed any lasting joy.

What about the person who seeks for fulfillment in relationships with other people? Whether it is friendship or a romantic relationship, friends and lovers can disappoint you. Nothing is more devastating than to be rejected by someone you care about. If things don't work out the way you think they ought to, does it necessarily mean your chance for happiness is gone? Of course not. But the people who base their happiness and self-esteem totally on relationships will be made to feel that way.

A difference exists between a fleeting happiness and long-lasting joy. If a person indulges the whim of temporary pleasure to the exclusion of something more substantial, he is bound to be disappointed with life. What I am asserting to you is it is possible to have joy regardless of the circumstances in life.

What is it then that produces that kind of joy? I believe some combination of the following five factors is essential to maintaining joy:

1. <u>Having a relationship</u> - Although you cannot base your joy totally on how others receive you, interaction with others is essential to our emotional well-being.
2. <u>A sense of accomplishment</u> - We need to feel that we are actually accomplishing something.
3. <u>A sense of righteousness</u> - Or (at the risk of sounding corny) wholesomeness
4. <u>Love</u>
5. <u>Having an absolute</u> - Something solid and dependable, whether creed or philosophy of life, that you can base your entire life on.

When, from the Upper Room, Jesus said, **"These things have I spoken unto you, that my joy might remain in you, and that your joy might be full,"** he specifically addressed each of these conditions. His desire for his disciples was that they would be filled with joy. To understand how joy is possible in the middle of our trial, we need to examine the words he spoke addressing each of these essentials. We will find in his words the keys we need to unlock a life full of joy.

HAVING A RELATIONSHIP

"Abide in me, and I in you."

Man is a social creature. He has an inbred need to fellowship and have interaction with others just like himself. It is only natural. People will go to great lengths developing relationships, which may turn out to be very tenuous, yet completely ignore the most satisfying and vital relationship, which is guaranteed to be everlasting.

The first essential to knowing joy is a vibrant, growing relationship with Jesus Christ.

Jesus said of the relationship between his disciples and himself, **"I am the vine, ye are the branches."** Our relationship with him is just as vital and necessary as a branch dependent on the vine for its very existence. It is no exaggeration to say *the basis of our joy is our relationship with the vine*. In fact, the other four factors contributing to our joy spring from this one. If this one is out of whack, everything else will be.

Using this analogy, we can say *the vine is our source of life.* As a branch receives its nourishment flowing from the vine, so we receive our health, strength, and very existence from Christ.

I believe, first of all, this refers to our physical life. In his sermon on Mars Hill in Athens recorded in Acts chapter 17, the Apostle Paul said of the Lord, **"In him we live, move, and have our being"** (verse 28). Our very life's breath is in the hands of God. Life is sacred because of its source. In the beginning, God breathed into man, and he became a living soul.

I also believe it can be applied to our spiritual life. At one time, I was spiritually dead. I could not understand spiritual matters. There was no life, no joy, and no purpose. There was a great emptiness or void within me. I needed a spiritual birth.

Then I met Jesus. HE BREATHED LIFE INTO ME. I was spiritually born into the family of God and now have the privilege of having fellowship with my Creator. Before he came, there was an empty spot in my life. After he came, it was a source of great joy.

If you are wondering why this relationship is so very vital, let me tell you what it meant to me. It means *I am never alone.* There will always be someone around who loves me.

I can remember one particular day when I was feeling extremely low. I was discouraged and depressed about several things that had transpired. I was driving down the road and began pouring out my complaint to the Lord in prayer. I was talking to the Lord, saying, "Lord, it just doesn't seem fair. Everything I try to do, I find myself standing alone. I try to do right, and there is no one who helps me. Lord, I AM ALL ALONE."

In my car, driving down Interstate 75, the Lord spoke to my heart so very clearly as if to say, "All right, hotshot. If you're so very 'all alone,' then *who in the world are you talking to?*"

That simple realization swept through me in an instant, bringing tears to my eyes and joy to my heart. I thought I was all alone but had been talking to him the whole time. I suppose if any driver had looked in my car, they would have thought I had gone completely nuts, but my discouragement had been instantly turned to rejoicing as I drove on in his presence.

The most important relationship in my life is that with Jesus Christ.

A SENSE OF ACCOMPLISHMENT

Fruit Bearing

"What am I doing here? Am I really worth anything? What am I actually accomplishing with my life?"

To many men, their self-worth is measured by what they can accomplish. That is why so many of them are bound emotionally to their jobs. Even if it is a job they are not particularly fond of, if they can feel like they are "doing" something, it will be personally fulfilling. That is also why losing a job can be so devastating to some. Without that sense of accomplishing something, a man will feel worthless, and life seems merely an existence.

Using the same imagery of the vine and branches, Jesus called this need to accomplish "bearing fruit." Another phrase that would describe fruit bearing would be *producing something in our lives*. Producing fruit will also produce joy and fulfillment.

There is a major difference, however, between the fruit the Lord was referring to and the general need to just achieve something. He referred to a very definite, specific type of fruit. To be quite honest, some of the things the world sees as achievement have little value, particularly if it exists strictly to feed our need for pleasure. Jesus spoke of fruit that was lasting in nature.

Scripture indicates there are two types of fruit found in a Christian. Galatians 5:22–23 speaks of the fruit of the Spirit as being love, joy, peace, patience, kindness, goodness, faith, gentleness, and self-control. This is the work the Spirit performs *within* the Christian. As we grow in grace and yield to his control, the Spirit develops these characteristics in us. It is an ongoing work, which strictly belongs to the Holy Spirit.

There is another type of fruit. Over and over in scripture, fruit will represent the works we do (some examples are found in Matt. 3:8, 7:15–20 and 2 Cor. 9:10). A person who has a relationship with the vine, a true branch, *will* produce some kind of fruit. We are saved by grace, not the works that we do, but a life that has been changed is bound to produce. A man will be marked by the deed that he does.

What is the fruit of a Christian? Whatever we do that effects other people in a positive way is the fruit of a genuine Christian. *This fruit is not for self-consumption.* You never see a branch eat its own fruit. The fruit is there for someone else to pick and eat. That being the case, let's look at some specific illustrations of fruit bearing.

The soul winner who leads a soul to faith in Christ has produced fruit that will last through eternity. This is probably the most tangible example for to some extent it is measurable. There is other fruit that is not quite so obvious.

Every act of kindness performed for no apparent reason is fruit. When you see someone who is hurting and you try to reach out and touch them, it is fruit, even if at the moment you feel your response is inadequate. When you perform an act of service that seems small and unnoticeable, it is fruit that can produce. I say these examples are less obvious because you may not see immediate results, but action like this paints the perfect picture of the compassion of Christ. People can see Christ illustrated in our lives, and it can have a positive effect on them that we may never see.

Not only can deeds affect others, but it is also fruit that multiples itself. There is an *ongoing production of fruit.* Fruit reproduces itself. When someone else picks and consumes the fruit we have produced, two things occur. The person finds nourishment in the fruit. He is strengthened and satisfied. Then, inside the fruit, he will find seeds. These seeds help him produce additional fruit. He is literally able to produce fruit because he has been helped or nourished by the fruit in our lives.

That is what it really means to accomplish something with your life, and there is a tremendous amount of satisfaction found in helping others. It is a certain source of joy.

Let me make one final point about fruit bearing. *The bearing of fruit by the branch is dependent upon the vine.* Unless the branch is connected to the vine, it has no source of nourishment to produce fruit. This goes back to our relationship with Christ. We cannot produce these kinds of deeds without Christ. Jesus had said to the disciples, **"As the branch cannot bear fruit of itself, except it abide in the vine; no more can ye, except ye abide in me."** If we are not growing in our walk with the Lord or if something such as sin hinders our fellowship with Jesus, we will not produce fruit, and our joy will be affected.

But if we are growing in our personal relationship with him and are bearing fruit that reproduces itself, an abundance of joy will flood our hearts. Life is then very good and extremely satisfying. Life is worth living.

A SENSE OF RIGHTNESS OR WHOLESOMENESS

Cleansing

One of the things that make children so endearing to us is their innocence. They are totally dependent on adults and very trusting, and they have not been hardened by life.

Disillusionment comes with the loss of innocence. When a person loses his innocence, there is an overwhelming feeling that something just isn't "right." Things are not as we imagined them to be. This is what happens in many marriages. A couple enters marriage with certain unrealistic expectations and finds things don't always work according to their preconceived notions.

Some of this is a natural part of maturing, of "growing up." Sometimes, however, it can be identified as a loss of purity, which can, without question, have a devastating effect on our emotional well-being and, therefore, our contentment.

Here enters the little three-letter word whose very existence is challenged by the world. It is the little word SIN.

Whatever happened to sin? It is not popular today to speak about the concept of sin. Psychologists will try to deny the existence of sin and say there is no reason to feel guilty about anything. Anyone who speaks about sin will be labeled a "wild-eyed, religious nut."

At the risk of being labeled a "nut," let me affirm to you that there is such a thing as sin. All one has to do is read the newspaper to see the result of sin.

The nature of sin is it is destructive. It destroys all it touches. It may harm your physical body, destroy relationships so vital to our well-being, or devastate a person's emotional stability.

Nothing will disrupt our contentment in life more than sin. Often the very thing that upsets us so can be traced back and identified as a natural result of some of our own actions. We generally do not like to admit this, so we play the blame game. We shift the blame elsewhere. "I wasn't responsible for my actions. Something or someone else caused me to do it."

The reason people will not accept responsibility for their actions is they must feel that they are "right." So to justify their actions, they rationalize things away. Unfortunately, by doing this, the root cause of their discontentment is never dealt with, and the seeds of destruction are left to grow to fruition.

In order for a Christian's joy to flourish unchecked, he must know he has been cleansed from his sin and there is nothing to come between him and his Lord.

How does a person stay pure in an impure world? Jesus said to his disciples, **"Now ye are clean through the word which I have spoken unto you. Abide in me, and I in you."**

The Word of God is alive. It is a living book. It is essential to my spiritual growth and the relationship I am building with the Lord Jesus. As I read and study God's Word, I take it in and ingest it. I feed on it until it becomes a part of me. I let it shape my life. I choose its precepts as the guiding principles of my life.

As I store up the Word of God, it becomes my buffer against sin. Let me be quick to add it is not a defensive weapon. Ephesians 6:17 refers to it as the sword of the Spirit—an offensive weapon. To stay clean, we need to be daily in God's Word and then when temptation arises, we need to attack it with the Word of God.

This daily devotion time enables us as Jesus commanded his disciples to "abide in him." Here is double protection. The Word protects us, and his continuous presence restrains us.

I cannot reemphasize strongly enough that impurity *will* disrupt our joy, but knowing all is well between my Savior and me and that there is nothing hindering my walk with him is the very source of the deepest joy.

LOVE

"Continue Ye in My Love"

Everybody talks about love. Its virtues always seem to be trumpeted in the current music, books, and movies. They all try to say their version of love is the answer.

The only problem is the world's love turns out to be temporary. It has no sticking power. It seems to be "love for the moment," and when that moment is gone, they move on to the next object of infatuation.

I believe the problem is people do not have a clue what love actually is. In chapter 2, I have already dealt with the Savior's love, so I will not go into a lot of detail about it here. In simplistic terms, love is *giving of yourself.*

Jesus's word about it to the disciples was, **"As the Father hath loved me, so I have loved you: continue ye in my love."** These words suggest the following pattern: an example set and an example followed.

This love originates with the Father who sets the example for the Son. He literally gave the darling of his heart, the most precious thing in Heaven, when he sent his Son into the world. This is *the* shining example of giving.

The Son, in submission to the Father, takes that example and follows it by constantly giving himself for others throughout his entire lifetime. In fact, when he spoke these words, he was about to give himself on a cross for the sins of the world. This is *the ultimate* gift.

Then he said to his disciples, "As I have given you an example of love, you are to take that example, follow it, and continue in my love." To continue in his love would mean a continuous giving of themselves even as Jesus gave of himself. It would mean the needs of others would always come before their own. To follow his example of love would mean they would not pursue their own dreams but would be in submission to God's will.

When we read history, we find the disciples were obedient to this command. They gave of themselves unselfishly, even unto death. By doing so, the gospel spread, and it eventually became possible for us to hear the life-changing message of salvation. Something else happened as well. They became heroes of the faith. By reading of their faithfulness, we become inspired to attempt great things for the Lord. This is *the goal of love*—to reproduce itself.

Not everyone you show love to will reciprocate. Unfortunately, some will shun it and treat you spitefully. But to show God's love by giving, expecting nothing in return, will bring other joys. And if you do it faithfully enough, somewhere someone will take notice and begin following your example.

And the gift of love will continue on and on and on.

HAVING AN ABSOLUTE

"Keep My Commandments"

We live in a world that thinks there are no absolutes. Everything is relative. There is no clear cut right and wrong, only "shades" of right. It is left up to the individual to determine what is right for himself, or so the world says.

Freedom to decide is essential to our concept of liberty. God recognizes freedom to choose in that he gave man a free will.

Let me make a distinction here. Free will does not mean man has the right to decide what is right and wrong. It means he has the right to *choose to do right* or reject what is right.

An absolute standard of right and wrong exists that man must abide by if he is to live peaceably and with true joy. It is a standard that does not depend upon the whims of man. If you were to quiz any group of ten people or more about any given subject, you would probably get as many different ideas as there are people in the group. Because human beings are so different, with so many different viewpoints, God gives us a standard of right and wrong to go by. It is the standard of his Word.

When people try to order their lives without something rock-solid to ground upon, they will end up with one of two things: the feeling of being adrift or anarchy.

There is no more unsettling feeling than that of being *adrift*. It is like floating down a river on a raft without a paddle. You have no control over where you are going. You are at the mercy of the river current. Up ahead are rocks and rapids, but you are helpless to steer.

Without God's rock-solid Word to depend upon, your life is adrift. The philosophy of "amorality," the idea that there is no clear cut right or wrong, leaves you helpless in the stream. How do I make decisions? Where do I go from here? What is right for me? Is it any wonder there is little joy when life is in such an unsettled condition?

Stability comes when you recognize God's standard, and you are obedient to his command to **"keep my commandments."**

If every man becomes a law within himself, when he does what is right in his own eyes, then we end up with *anarchy*. In a state of anarchy, a person will become a servant to his own self-interest. Unfortunately, in reaching for the things he desires, other people's interests may get in the way. To get ahead, you must infringe upon the other person's rights. Likewise, others may prevent you from reaching your goal.

Without a solid governing standard to go by, the law of the jungle prevails. The resulting chaos effectively wipes out the environment there is in living.

Order is the result when God's standard is obeyed. Having an absolute standard to govern our lives is essential to experiencing joy. What some would consider restrictive is actually intended to better our existence. The *stability and order* that is the result of keeping God's commandments creates the proper atmosphere in which we can successfully build our lives so that *joy may prosper*.

* * * * *

Where is joy found?

Jesus spoke very clearly to the disciples. He said joy would be found in their relationship with him and by the fruit that would spring up in their lives through that relationship. As others would benefit from the fruit in their lives, joy would multiply, and they would experience a love more satisfying than anything they could imagine. The purity in their lives and their obedience to his commandments would maintain that relationship, insuring that joy would continue to grow.

Does this mean they would never have a difficult time? No way. In fact, some of them would pay dearly for their faith.

Our path to joy will be the same as for the disciples. If we want that inner joy that always abides, we need to pay attention to those words coming from the Upper Room. They will lead us to a life full of blessings that are both unbelievable and indescribable.

But do not think the path will be easy. Just like the disciples, we may stumble over some rocks in our path. The way may not be smooth. One needs only to see how the work of the Father is portrayed in the words of Jesus to see this clearly.

Jesus called the Father the husbandman (the gardener) and said **"every branch that beareth fruit, he purgeth it** (prunes it)**, that it may bring forth more fruit."** The process of pruning is not enjoyable, but it is necessary to bearing fruit. There are things that get in the way and hinder the production of fruit. They must be removed in order to insure a good crop.

We may not even realize it, but there may be things in our lives that are actually hindering our walk with Christ. The Father, in love, sends us through a pruning experience designed to take away what is useless and cumbersome in our lives. We may not understand at the time why we are going through these difficulties, but do not lose heart. He is cutting back the things that hinder our growth and taking away every trait that is unlike Jesus. He is striving to conform us to the image of his Son.

The Father's view of the branches is this: *he expects normalcy.* It is normal and expected that if a branch is connected to the vine, *it will bring forth fruit.* Not to bring forth fruit is abnormal.

God's love has allowed every difficulty we face to come our way. Through them, we grow and produce fruit. And through the production of fruit, there is joy.

The Scripture
THE NEW RELATIONSHIP

"Henceforth I call you not servants; for the servant knoweth not what his Lord doeth: but I have called you friends; for all things that I have heard of my Father I have made known unto you.

Ye have not chosen me, but I have chosen you, and ordained you, that ye should go and bring forth fruit, and that your fruit should remain; and whatsoever ye shall ask of the Father in my name, he may give it to you.

These things I command you, that you love one another."

—John 15:15–17

Chapter *11*

THE NEW RELATIONSHIP

I can remember the first time the phrase "being saved" registered in my mind. I was seven years old at the time.

My brother John, two years older than I, had gone to a revival meeting with my grandparents and had just gotten home with some thrilling news.

I was in bed, drifting in that twilight between sleep and wakefulness. Johnny came running excitedly into the room saying, "Jimmy, I got saved tonight!"

I was only seven and didn't really know what he was talking about. Besides which, I never have exactly been my sharpest when I first wake up. I thought maybe someone had pulled him out of the path of a speeding car or something of that nature. I groggily asked, "Who saved you?"

Johnny thought I was making fun of him and stomped out the room. I could hear my parents in the next room explaining to him, "Jimmy's still very young. He doesn't understand."

Me? I just rolled over and went back to sleep.

I was suffering from a common illusion. I wish I could say it was because I was just a child and did not know any better, but I have found many full-grown adults who cling to the same illusion.

I thought I had Heaven made because of who I was. My granddaddy was a preacher—the pastor of our church. My parents were as good a Christian couple as there could be. I would never have done some of the things my friends did. I always tried to be a good little boy, and I had *always* believed in Jesus. Certainly, if anyone was going to Heaven then, I was.

But it was still just an illusion. I had never had a born-again experience. I thought who I was made me a Christian. A good definition of self-righteousness is "depending upon yourself for your righteousness," and from that viewpoint, I was self-righteous.

The problem with self-righteousness is it places all the emphasis on *me* and overlooks two important facts. First, it overlooks the inability of man to make himself righteous. Then, it overlooks the fact that God's provision for my salvation *was not me*. If a person considers himself righteous on his own merits, he will miss what God has provided for our forgiveness. In the final analysis, self-righteousness is as great a sin as any, whether it is found in a child or an adult.

It really didn't make that huge an impact on me that night, but for the first time, it entered my mind that there was just something missing. I slowly began to realize I could not depend on my granddaddy or anyone else in my family to take me to Heaven. I didn't quite realize it yet, but I had come to Jesus on my own.

For three years, I struggled with my need to be saved, and I hit upon a convenient excuse: "I don't understand." If the question of salvation ever came up, I would draw that excuse like a gun, and believe me I, became a quick draw. I claimed I did not understand, but the truth was I understood a lot more than I let on.

I was going through what the old country churches called "Holy Ghost conviction." What was happening inside me was exactly what we talked about in chapter 9. The Holy Spirit was convincing me of my need for Jesus.

A discomforting pattern developed during church service that anyone who has been through Holy Ghost conviction can identify with. To get a clear picture of it, I will need to describe the way the Chattahoochee Baptist Church building was laid out.

In Chattahoochee's old building, the choir pews were not directly behind the pulpit. To the right of the pulpit were the adult choir pews. To the left of the pulpit were the young people's choir pews. They did not look out toward the congregation but was on either side of the pulpit, facing each other. My parents would sit in the adult choir, and I would sit with the other children and youth in the youth choir.

During the preaching, I would busy myself drawing pictures, writing notes, or doing most anything to keep from hearing the sermon. I would do all right throughout most of the service, but *then* the INVITATION would come and it would tear me out of the frame.

My parents were very concerned for me. When the invitation was given, my mom, who was sitting directly across from me, would begin staring at me with tears in her eyes. She had such a burden for me that she literally would be weeping, wanting to see me get saved. Her gaze was almost more than I could stand. I would try almost anything to get away from it. I would scoot down the pew to position the pulpit between Mom and me so I wouldn't have to see her. If there were other children in the way, I would push them down the bench, and you would see an entire bench of children scooting. Anything to escape that look.

This went on for quite a while. It was obvious the Lord was dealing with me, but if anyone tried to speak to me about it, I would shoot down the conversation with the same old excuse: "I'm confused. I don't understand."

March 29, 1964, dawned a very beautiful sunny day. It was Easter Sunday. As was the practice on Easter, Mom had us kids all decked out in brand new outfits. I had me a neat little suit with a bow tie. I was sporting a fresh haircut. It was what I used to call a "baby bird" haircut because I thought it made me look like a baby bird. I was looking real "spiffy."

I remember walking outside to get in the car to go to church. I looked up the street and saw one of my friends outside in his play clothes throwing a stick with his dog. I thought, "I'm going to church, and he isn't. I'm better than he is."

Yes, I really thought that. In spite of the Holy Spirit's work in my life, I was still trying to think *who I was* qualified me for Heaven. Even when found in a cute little ten-year-old boy all decked out for Easter, self-righteousness sounds terribly arrogant.

That Sunday morning, the service followed the usual pattern. I would draw during the sermon and try to avoid Mom's stare during the invitation. I was getting pretty adept at escaping her gaze, but I couldn't escape a certain impression—a still small voice speaking ever louder and with more urgency to my heart. I know now it was God moving upon my heart, trying to draw me into a relationship with him. Unfortunately, I was also getting pretty adept at saying no. I did not respond.

That evening, Easter Sunday night, began our Spring Revival at Chattahoochee. Rev. Ben Turner was the visiting preacher. That evening was different.

Ben Turner was a young version of the old-time preacher man. He preached with fire *and* content. I'm not sure I remember all he preached on, but something was going on in my heart.

Chattahoochee had an old-fashioned altar or mourner's bench. When the invitation was given, the altar filled up with people kneeling in prayer. Some people were praying for revival. Some were praying for lost friends. I think my entire family was at the altar praying. They were praying for me.

I was miserable. I could literally feel my heart thumping in my chest. I don't know how to describe the feeling. It was similar to a scared feeling, but it was more like the feeling I had when my dad would lecture or punish me for doing wrong. It would break my heart to think Dad was disappointed in me. That's the way I felt then, but I hadn't done anything to disappoint Dad. My heart was breaking, and I didn't understand why. Why should I feel that way?

I felt that way because I was guilty and knew it. I knew I needed Jesus.

Sometime around the third or fourth verse, my brother Johnny walked over to me and put his arm around me. He was crying. He said something like, "Jimmy, don't you want to be saved?" At that instant, the Holy Spirit broke through my will. I found myself kneeling at the altar with my parents and grandparents around me.

You may have seen or heard many versions of what is referred to as the sinner's prayer. I was a ten-year-old boy and didn't know how to pray very well. I prayed the only thing I knew to pray. I basically prayed a three word sinner's prayer, "Lord, save me." That's the only thing I remember saying.

An instantaneous, unmistakable change happened within me. That heavy burden was gone. I felt clean and brand new inside. The first words out of my mouth were, "It's wonderful!" The very instant I trusted him, I knew things would never be the same.

Jesus had come into my heart. I was a different little boy.

That's how I entered into this relationship.

In the years following, I've heard some Christians question the validity of childhood professions of faith. One specific instance comes to my mind.

I went out witnessing for the church one day with a man I had never gone out visiting with before. As it turned out, he did most of the talking.

We were talking with a young couple in their driveway, and he asked the lady if she had ever received the Lord as her Savior. She immediately replied, "Oh, yes! I was saved when I was ten years old."

He then countered with, "Oh, I don't believe a person can really understand what they are doing when they are that young." He then proceeded to try and convince the lady she was lost and needed to be saved.

He was shocked later on in the car to find out I had been saved at that very same age. He kept on asking, "Are you sure?"

Does a ten-year-old understand what he is doing? Did I understand what I was doing? I was ten years old. I understood what a ten year old understands. At the time, I probably could not have given you a definition of repentance, faith, or salvation. But let me tell you what I *did* understand.

I knew I was lost.

I knew I couldn't save myself.

I had heard the man of God preach the Gospel: that Jesus died, was buried, and raised again to save us from our sins.

I knew the Holy Spirit was doing a number on my heart.

I knew the instant I trusted him with a childlike faith that he saved me. No question about it.

At the time I am writing this, it has been fifty-three years since that day I accepted Jesus as my Savior. The answer I gave that well-intentioned man is the same today as it was then. Am I sure? "I am absolutely positive. There's no doubt about it. Jesus Christ has changed my life."

Since that day in 1964, I have had a genuine, *growing relationship* with Jesus Christ.

I have a friend.

* * * * *

In the Upper Room, Jesus said to his disciples, "Our relationship is going to change. Until now, our bond has been one of master/servant, and even though it is as it should be, from now on, I will call you my *friends*."

Jesus deserves to be called Master. His holiness requires our obedience, adoration, and worship. We ought to consider it the highest honor just to be called his servant.

But Jesus wants much more from his children than just obeying him out of a sense of duty. He wants it to be a *loving, growing relationship* where his children spend enough time with him to consider him more than just a passing acquaintance. He wants to be our dearest friend.

Who is the friend you talk to when facing a storm? Who is the one you would rather spend time with than anyone else you know? Who is the friend you would trust with your life?

Jesus wants to be that friend. Whereas our human friendships are very important, cultivating this divine friendship is essential to our spiritual and emotional well-being.

Desiring to have this kind of relationship with us *Jesus made the first move*. He stepped out from eternity and came into our world. He made it possible for us to see what God was like. And he is the one who first called us friends.

He instigated the relationship. That is why he could say, **"Ye have not chosen me, but I have chosen you."** The question now is how will we respond to what he initiated?

I firmly believe a lot of the struggles we have would be a lot easier to handle if our relationship with the Lord was as strong as it should be. What should our relationship with him be like?

HOW SHOULD THIS FRIENDSHIP BE CHARACTERIZED?

How do you describe a friendship? We have already indicated that it should be a *growing relationship*. We should never let it stagnate. To keep it vibrant and of primary importance to us requires effort. Like anything else we need to work at keeping it fresh. This means spending time with him, seeking to discover more about his nature. It should be a labor of love, from one adoring heart to another.

Our friendship with him ought to be characterized as a *sharing relationship*, and sharing is a two-way street.

Let us first look at how Jesus shares with us. Jesus essentially told his disciples that a slave doesn't know what his master is doing but went on to say, **"I have called you friends; for all things that I have heard of my Father I have made known unto you."** Jesus shares with us the heart of God.

We will never know all that God knows, but through our friendship with Christ, we will catch a glimpse of God's heart. We will be able to sense the love and compassion that motivates him. We will begin to understand the holiness of his nature that abhors sin. The more time we spend with him, some of his nature should rub off on us. We should be moved more compassionately. The more time we spend in his holiness, the more we should be repulsed by sin and degradation, even that which we find buried deep inside us.

As we see more of him and yield to his influence, he begins to conform us to the image of his Son, and in that way, his heart can be shared with us.

He also shares with us in that he reveals to us his will for our lives. There is a path he has marked for us. He desires the very best for us. The closer we get to him, the clearer the path is. His will is knowable. He shares his will with us.

No friendship can be strong if it is directed one-way. Not only must he share with us, but we must also share with him. We must give to him our hearts, our souls, and even our dreams. We must willingly surrender everything we are to him, and let him control every aspect of our lives.

After we have done that, there is another glorious way we share with him. We share our requests and needs with him, and he responds to it. He said, **"Whatever ye shall ask of the Father in my name, he may give it to you."** This is the sharing aspect of our relationship.

Next, we can say our friendship should be noted as a *relationship that brings out the best in ourselves.*

Some human relationships bring out baseness and perversity in a person. This is a wantonly destructive relationship. Any relation that does not promote goodness and wholesomeness should be avoided at all costs, no matter how much they claim to "love" you. If it inspires or draws wickedness out of you, then it is destructive.

Friendship with Jesus will draw the very best out of me. He told the disciples, **"I have chosen you, and ordained you, that ye should go and bring forth fruit."** The fruit of the Spirit we talked about in the last chapter, everything noble that can be found in a human being, is pulled out of us by the influence and the very presence of Jesus.

Not only can I accomplish things, but I can also *be* the very best person I can possibly be because of my relation with the Lord Jesus.

It is a new relationship made possible by his sacrifice on the cross for us.

Most of this book has been directed toward the person who already knows Jesus Christ as their Savior. There may be someone reading this, however, who has never settled this issue.

You may be experiencing a trial and have searched for some comfort, yet you have found none. It may very well be that you have never had this kind of relationship with God. You may have always believed in God and even prayed to him, but it seemed like you were praying to murals on a ceiling.

Let me ask you a question. Have you ever had a *born-again experience*? Jesus told Nicodemus in John 3:3, **"Except a man be born again, he cannot see the Kingdom of God."** He said, "Nicodemus, it is an absolute necessity!"

Before you can seek for comfort or help in the words of Jesus, this all-important matter must be forever settled.

Briefly, the "new birth" is a spiritual birth quite separate and apart from physical birth. Just as I was not a Christian because of who I was or who my family was, so everyone must of their own volition come to Christ and receive the Lord Jesus.

When a person *repents* of (turns from) their sins and receives *by faith* Jesus Christ as their Lord and Savior, then they are born spiritually and become a child of God. This is possible because Jesus died on the cross for my sins, was buried, and three days later rose from the grave.

Someone may say, "I don't understand that."

Does God require understanding or *faith*? I cannot think of a single scripture that demands we understand before we are saved, but scripture does require a *childlike faith*.

My prayer is if you have never been changed by the power of God, you will this very instant call upon the Lord and receive by faith his gift of eternal life. THEN you will find a friend who will never leave your side and will be a source of comfort to you during the trial of your life.

> **"For whosoever shall call upon the name of the Lord shall be saved."**
>
> —Romans 10:13

The Scripture

CORRECTING OUR PERSPECTIVE

"If the world hate you, ye know that it hated me before it hated you.

If ye were of the world, the world would love its own; but because ye are not of the world, but I have chosen you out of the world, therefore the world hateth you.

Remember the word that I said unto you, The servant is not greater than his lord. If they have persecuted me, they will also persecute you; if they have kept my saying, they will keep yours also.

But these things will they do unto you for my name's sake, because they know not him that sent me.

If I had not come and spoken unto them, they had not had sin; but now, they have no cloak for their sin.

He that hateth me hateth my Father also.

If I had not done among them the words which no other man did, they had not had sin; but now have they both seen and hated both me and my Father.

But this cometh to pass, that the word might be fulfilled that is written in their law, They hated me without a cause."

—John 15:18–25

Chapter *12*

CORRECTING OUR PERSPECTIVE

A king of antiquity went to battle. An enemy was advancing toward his kingdom. At stake was the safety of his subjects and their families.

He had a son who was destined for the throne, but he was untested in battle. The king decided that his son would lead his armies in defense of the kingdom.

As they stood on a hill overlooking a lush valley with their armies arrayed around them, they could see the approach of the enemy. It was an awesome sight. The son could not help but feel a little fear building up inside him.

The king turned to his son and began to speak, "If you would one day rule this people, you must learn to lead them in difficult circumstances. If you would have their loyalty, you must win it fairly. You must lead our armies into battle and earn the right to rule."

Outlining the plan of battle, the king continued, "I know this king. He is a crafty adversary. I will hold back part of our forces on this hill lest he try to encircle us and strike at the city. You will take the remainder and engage him in this valley."

Sensing his son's trepidation, he reassuringly added, "Do not fear. If you feel like the battle is not going well and you are about to be overrun, lift your sword high up into the air. I will be watching from the hill. If I see your sword raised, I will send these held in reserve to your aid."

So the son took charge of the armies and marched them toward the approaching swarm. There seemed to be so many of them, which only heightened his dread of the coming collision.

The battle ensued and was worse than he ever imagined it would be. He had never experienced anything so intense or gruesome as what he was facing now.

The struggle continued on into the late afternoon. It seemed like the enemy wouldn't stop coming. The only thing that kept him going was a rush of adrenalin, but exhaustion was gradually taking over. Was there no end to this?

At a crucial point in the battle, the king's son could sense nothing around him but the adversary. He thought, "This is it. The battle has turned against us, and we are about to be overrun."

He swung his sword, disarmed his present foe, and lifted his sword high up in the air until his next antagonist presented himself.

The battle continued. No one came.

"Perhaps," he thought, "my father did not see my sword lifted with such confusion all around." The next opportunity that came, he lifted his sword again.

Still no help came.

The battle wore on to early evening, till there was no more enemy coming at them. Totally drained, he nearly collapsed on the ground in fatigue.

Soon the king with his guard approached them as they rested on the field of battle.

The son, sitting on the ground, looked up at his father and said, "Where were you? Did you not see my sword? You have let me down."

The king softly replied, "Yes, I saw your sword raised, but I saw something else you could not see. Down in the valley, you could not see over the next hill. From my vantage point, I could see the other side. I saw there were no more armies there to fight. When you raised your sword, you already had the battle won and didn't even realize it. Had I intervened, I would have robbed you of the victory. People would have said, 'The king has won the victory.' As it is, the victory is yours."

He added, "From where you were, it seemed like you were losing the battle, but *your perspective was wrong.*"

* * * * *

We go through life with limited sight. We see things from one vantage point only: that of an earthbound individual.

Much of the frustration we experience is due to this fact. We try to serve the Lord but feel like we have been a failure. We try to do right, and it seems there is no one to take our side. We have tried to be an encouragement to others, yet when life deals us a tough hand, there is no one to lift us up.

Things are seldom as bleak as we view them.

The young man trying to serve the Lord may not see the impact he has had on others while in this life, but there is a Heavenly Father who is keeping account.

The person who takes a courageous stand for right may feel like he is standing alone. He may not have seen the ones who have gained courage to do right because of his example. His eyes cannot see the grandstands of Heaven rejoice and applaud his stand for truth and right.

The person who senses no one to lift him up may have had his vision clouded. There may be friends all around him anxious to help, but for some reason, he has shut them out.

What are some of the things that limit our vision?

For one thing, our vision has *limited ability.* There are just some things we are not able to see. We cannot read the heart of another individual. We really do not know what that person is thinking. We merely perceive what we "think" he is thinking, based on sensory input (what we can hear, action we see, etc.).

Our vision is also restricted to this physical world. There is a spiritual world just as real. With the physical eye, we do not see the multitudes of spiritual beings encamping around us. We may sense the effects of spiritual warfare, but we generally do not view angels or demons vying for the souls of men.

Since there are some things we just cannot see, how can we measure the impact our lives have had for the Kingdom of God? We may not in this life. That is why there is a coming day when God, who *is* all-seeing, shall reward the works of his children.

Sometimes our vision is *clouded by sorrow.* A person may be so overcome with grief that he cannot see through his own tears clearly. He does not see the mercy of God because he is overwhelmed by his grief.

There are times when the grieving process is necessary for our emotional well-being, as with the death of a loved one. But along with the grieving, there must be comfort.

We may also be blinded by *self-pity.* We WANT to feel sorry for ourselves and do not want to admit things are not so bad. Some people seem to have a natural disposition to have "pity-parties," where they can get together with themselves and sulk about how miserable they are. They are so wrapped up in pity they forget about all the people who really care for them.

I remember one particular time when I was going through a difficult time. I got to feeling sorry for myself and felt none of my friends had remembered me. I was left to fend for myself, and I just knew nobody cared.

Several months later, I was going through some things and came across a card someone had sent me. It basically said they knew things were tough at the moment, and they were praying for me.

I looked closely at the card and remembered it. It had been sent to me during the hard time when I felt like I had been forgotten. I had read it, somehow overlooked it, and continued to feel pity for myself. I just knew I had been forgotten during that time. But as it turned out, that was not the case, and here in my hand was the proof. How could I have missed it?

God had, through that person, sent me a note of encouragement. I was so blinded by my self-pity, however, that I just refused to see it. I had been so miserable through that entire time, and now God was revealing to me that it was self-imposed. I had allowed my feelings to limit my view, and I couldn't see the situation as it actually was.

These are just a few of the things that can cloud our vision. Any number of things can limit our perception in life.

When we allow our limited vision to discourage us, it is time to have our perspective corrected.

There was one specific type of circumstance Jesus had to address in the Upper Room. It was the fact that the disciples were going to experience persecution.

FACING PERSECUTION

Jesus understood *how* they viewed the coming persecution would influence their actions and help determine how well they would handle it. If they faced it as a personal attack, they would end up extremely discouraged or depressed. He, therefore, sought to correct their view. *He put things in perspective.*

More and more Christians in America are going to be facing persecution as American society runs further and further away from God's principles. We may not face death for our beliefs as the disciples did, but a Christian may receive "special treatment" in the work place. And I do not mean that in a positive way.

How will a Christian be treated in the work place? He will be told to keep his mouth shut concerning his faith. All subjects from sports to politics can be talked over during your break times, but to merely bring up the name of Jesus, unless it is in the context of swearing, is considered "unprofessional behavior." It just is not allowed.

Some supervisors may even make a Christian's life miserable. They have a position of authority, and there have been instances where they singled out an employee who is a believer.

Fellow workers may try their hand at it by using ridicule to laugh at the narrow Christian. We might even be made a scapegoat when something goes wrong.

Where the situation takes on a scary tone, however, is in the public domain. All references to God, religion, or Christianity have to be removed from public display for fear that it might offend someone or warp an adolescent. In effect, they are saying, "Keep your beliefs to yourself, and go hide in a corner with them. They have no place being aired publicly. You *have no right* to propagate your beliefs for that would be cramming it down someone's throat."

Where Christian faith is deemed to go against the "public interest," how big a step is it to actual physical persecution?

What did Jesus say to the disciples about facing persecution? He said basically four things.

He first spoke of the object of the persecution. *The object of the persecution of Christians is Jesus.* **"If the world hate you, ye know that it hated me before it hated you."** In effect, he said, "Their hatred is not really aimed at you. It is only directed at me."

It is only natural to take persecution personally as if it were an affront to me. This is the idea he is trying to correct. The world only hates us because of who we represent. Since they cannot physically see the Lord, they must strike out at the ones who are his representatives on Earth.

He then spoke of the fact that *Christians are different from the world.* We have a different citizenship. **"If ye were of the world, the world would love its own; but because ye are not of the world, but I have chosen you out of the world, therefore the world hateth you."**

They cannot understand us because we are different by nature. We have not only our sinful, human nature, but we have a spiritual nature born of God. That is what they cannot grasp and why they cannot comprehend why we are as we are. Anyone different from them, anything they cannot understand, THEY WILL HATE.

Someone might ask, "How could anyone treat Christians in such a way?" Jesus said the answer was because *they do not know God.*

"But these things will they do unto you for my name's sake, because they know not him that sent me."

Spiteful treatment from the world can be attributed to ignorance. Without knowledge of the truth, how can they understand what it means to "love one another?" They do not know how to live or act according to God's standard because they do not know him.

Finally, Jesus told the disciples *why the world would hate the Lord* and, because of our association with him, persecute the church. Jesus explained, **"If I had not come and spoken unto them, they had not had sin; but now, they have no cloak for their sin."**

The world was going along merrily, following its own path. All the while, they felt like they were always in the right, and if there were a God, certainly he must think as we do.

Then Jesus came on the scene. There's just something about purity and holiness that accentuates sinfulness. In Jesus, they saw God's standard, and it uncovered man as he really was. Every word and action of Jesus illuminated just how far short they came. *Jesus revealed their sinfulness*, and they came to realize they were sinners.

When confronted with this, a person can either repent of their sins, or they can reject it. Those that repent become believers. Those that reject it have to somehow justify themselves, and they may do it by lashing out at what has revealed their sin.

You have heard some people who so vehemently oppose Christianity that they are not satisfied merely to choose not to believe. They feel compelled to actively obstruct the free course of the gospel. They may even try to blame all the ills of the world on Christians or religion.

I believe this is their way of "whistling in the dark." The light of Christ has so stung them that, like a dog that has been bitten, they holler out loud.

Along comes the Christian who stands for what Christ stands for, and he is labeled ignorant, a loser, a hatemonger, or just plain sick. The offense of the cross has naturally been transferred to the child of God.

Jesus was trying to get the disciples to understand what was really happening when the world was persecuting them. He was trying to get them to view it correctly.

When we face persecution, we need to remember the exact same things and try to keep it all in perspective.

The world hates us because it hated Jesus.

We are different from the world.

They can persecute us without remorse because they don't know God.

They lash out at righteousness because it reveals their own wickedness.

THE NATURAL REACTION TO PERSECUTION

When a Christian is unfairly treated, he may understand the basis of persecution yet still react in a wrong way. At play here is human nature. It is only natural to think or feel a certain way when mistreated.

There are two problems with reacting to our gut instinct. First, we may find ourselves acting unchristian, certainly not Christlike. To follow the example left for us by Christ is one of our goals as a Christian. If we follow human nature, we have already lost for we have missed one of our basic goals: imitation of Christ. We may even find ourselves using the same tactics as our tormentors, conforming us to the image of the world rather than that of Christ. We become what we abhor.

The second problem is reacting according to human nature can lead to frustration for the actions we take may deepen the conflict. There is no guarantee that human devices will relieve the pressure.

How does human nature react to persecution? It might take one of four forms.

The first reaction usually is to *defend yourself*. You fight back to preserve your rights. Your only thought is to clear yourself, particularly in the case of slander.

The problem is when you set out to defend yourself, it usually draws even more vicious attacks from your antagonist. It seldom solves the problem.

This is usually followed by *anger*. You have been wronged, and it really has your "Irish" up. All of a sudden, new thoughts come to your mind. It will creep up on you subtly. You'll find yourself saying, "I'll remember this. Someday, I'll get him back. I can't let him get away with this." At this point, it's beginning to sound like revenge or a desire to reach out and hurt them.

When we let our anger take over, we find ourselves on their level using their tactics.

Anger clouds our judgment. We seldom think clearly when we are mad. When my brother and I were playing baseball, Dad used to say to us, "If the other team is needling you, ignore it, and go about your business. If they can ever get you mad, they have you beat. You can't think straight or concentrate on what you're doing if you're mad."

The same may be said about facing persecution. If you become so preoccupied with anger or with defending yourself, you will find yourself distracted from what you are trying to accomplish. If you get angry, they have you beat.

Your initial response may then be followed by *depression*. You begin to think, "Why in the world have they attacked *me?* What is there about me that is so bad that people will treat me this way?" You begin to take it personally.

Depression can then cause you to *question God*. You find yourself saying, "I don't understand this. I've tried to do right and all this happens. God, why did you let this happen to me?" Your faith is affected.

This is the natural way to respond, but it is the incorrect way to respond.

How then can I correct my perspective?

ADJUSTING YOUR VIEW

If I am going to respond right, I must think right. That means how I view things is all important.

Let me give you a *seven-point attitude adjustment* to follow. When facing persecution, try to do the following:

1.   *Examine yourself.* This may be difficult to do, but earnestly examine your own actions in the matter. Are you completely innocent in the matter, or has some action of yours brought it on? Remember, only things suffered for the sake

of Christ can be considered persecution. Otherwise, it is something you have earned.

2. *Don't take it personally.* Remember whom they are really attacking. It is not you personally. It is who you represent, and HE will take it personally and take your case.

3. *Don't expect the world to act like Christians.* They are not. You will only be frustrated unless you understand they are acting the only way they know how, as people without God.

4. *Don't view them as your enemy.* Remember Ephesians 6:12. It is not flesh and blood we fight against. They are not the enemy. The enemy is the spiritual powers that influence them.

5. *Don't try to strike back.* You will only do more damage to yourself by adopting their means.

6. *Place it in God's hands.* Let him handle it as he sees fit. Remember, there is a law of sowing and reaping. Whatever a man sows that he shall reap. If they have wronged you spiritually without a cause, it will be visited back upon them without you dirtying your hands in it. Let the Lord fight that battle for you.

7. *Do good to them who mistreat you.* This really does require a lot of grace. But if we are followers of him, we need to follow his instructions found in Matthew 5:44–45: **"But I say unto you, Love your enemies, bless them that curse you, do good to them that hate you, and pray for them which despitefully use you, and persecute you; that ye may be the children of your Father which is in heaven."**

When I was young in the ministry, an older preacher once told me, "If it ever seems everyone is always kicking you in the rear, it just means you are way out in front of them."

That may be a different way to phrase it, but it is generally true that the person who is doing something for Christ and accomplishing something is the one who will be persecuted. The person accomplishing nothing will be left alone.

If you ever take up the cause and take a stand for the Lord Jesus Christ, you will become a target. There *is* an adversary out there, the Devil, who will not let you go unchallenged.

Instead of letting it get you down, you ought to consider it a compliment that you have been singled out for persecution. It just means they have seen enough of Christ about you to know you are a Christian. Rejoice that you are considered worthy to face persecution for we know we are in the hands of a merciful God.

> **"Indeed we count them blessed who endure. You have heard of the perseverance of Job and see the end intended by the Lord—that the Lord is very compassionate and merciful."**
>
> —James 5:11 (NKJV)

The Scripture

BEYOND WEEPING

"Now Jesus knew that they were desirous to ask him, and said unto them, Do you inquire among yourselves of what I said, A little while, and ye shall not see me; and again, a little while, and ye shall see me?

Verily, verily, I say unto you, Ye shall weep and lament, but the world shall rejoice; and ye shall be sorrowful, but your sorrow shall be turned into joy.

A woman, when she is in travail, hateth sorrow, because her hour is come; but as soon as she is delivered of the child, she remembereth no more the anguish, for joy that a man is born into the world.

And ye now, therefore, have sorrow; but I will see you again, and your heart shall rejoice, and your joy no man taketh from you."

—John 16:19–22

Chapter *13*

BEYOND WEEPING

My Eddy

"From his garden in the sky
God sent me a little rose.
He entrusted in me the care
Of a dear little bud he chose.

Somehow my flower was broken
When he came down from above,
But though my rose was not perfect,
He was sweet and so easy to love.

Time and again I did wonder
What did I do so wrong?
Then God sent another rosebud;
Big and healthy and strong.

I need not know the reason.
I just need to trust and pray
That He will mend my flower

When I take him back home someday."

—Myra Foster

I opened up the book. It was beginning to show some age. The white cover seemed a little more dingy. The pages were a little more yellowed. It had that "stored" feel. It must have been thirty years since I had looked through the book.

The first few pages told the story: "In Loving Memory - Eddy Lee Foster." I turned the page, and there were the newspaper clippings. I read each one of them. The headline of one read, "JOBO FOSTER LOSES THIRTEEN-YEAR-OLD SON."

I turned the next page, and there was a single rose pressed between the pages. Its bright red color had been turned very dark, nearly black, by the passage of thirty-two years. I remembered Mom's caution as she lent me the book. "Don't lose my rose."

Page after page, I turned, and with each page, memory after memory tumbled over one another. There were listed the names of long-time friends of the family I had not thought about for years. There, too, in that list of family members was a pet name Mom had for Dad that had nearly eluded my memory: "Daddy-Buddy."

There was another memory from childhood awakened. It was the memory of a very special little boy whose presence blessed our family and held such an impact on the bond of love we felt.

Eddy was my brother. He was born in 1950, three years and five months prior to me.

When Eddy was born, something went terribly wrong. For some reason, he couldn't breathe for several minutes. As a result, there was extensive brain damage. Because of his condition, he was not expected to live a normal life span.

Eddy would live to be thirteen years of age. During his life, he was never able to walk or even sit up. Except when he was being held or carried, he would spend the day lying on his stomach. As a result of disuse, his muscles atrophied, and his entire body became very rigid.

Eddy was never able to speak. He was not able to communicate by ordinary means, but there was one thing he would respond to: love. At times, when Dad or Mom would be holding him and speaking to him so lovingly, he would look them in the eyes, and you could tell it reached him. He may not have been able to understand or articulate words, but it was as if he was trying his best to communicate love back.

Many people would have viewed Eddy's affliction as a tragedy, and certainly it must have been heartbreaking for Mom and Dad that their first child was not healthy. But looking back on my childhood days, I never remembered any hint of disappointment from my parents. What I do remember is their loving care of Eddy. He was their son, and they loved him so.

I watched them as they juggled a hectic schedule. With two other sons playing little league baseball, work schedules, church, and taking care of Eddy, it was a tremendous undertaking. Not every couple would have had the grace to handle it, but my parents did because they loved all three of us kids.

People helped along the way. There was our housekeeper, Mrs. Rebecca Castle, who was so good with Eddy. There was the church family that was always there. All were blessings sent from God to help as Mom and Dad cared for their special son.

As I turned the next page, I found a poem Mom had written about Eddy before I was born. As I read it, I could sense something of their heartbreak over their "broken rose" yet saw their love for Eddy displayed right alongside of it.

I was in bed asleep when Eddy passed away. I vaguely remember hearing Mom speaking to Dad in the next room as if from a great distance. There was an obvious note of distress in her voice. I drifted back off to sleep again.

The next thing I remember, I was awakened by Johnny coming into the bedroom. He was crying and said, "Eddy's dead."

I didn't believe him. I got up and went running into the living room.

When I got to the door of the living room, I stopped dead still. Some friends of the family, Junior and Mildred Smith, were there. They had been speaking in hushed tones till they saw me, then they got quiet. No one needed to say a word to me. I instantly knew. I turned and went running back to my bed crying.

As I was leafing through these pages thirty-two years later, the memories, along with their accompanying feelings, were awakened. They still seemed as vivid as they were that night.

The next turn on the page uncovered another poem my mom had written on the very day of the funeral.

I Gave My Boy Back to Jesus Today
"I gave my boy back to Jesus today;
The one he had loaned me in his wee house of clay.
But Jesus was with me when I bid him adieu,
With birds sweetly singing and the sky so deep blue.
In so many ways he made the parting so sweet,
When friends and dear loved ones at the church house did meet;
With the fragrance of flowers of all different hues,
And the sound of sweet music drifting out o're the pews.
And the words that he gave the preacher to say
Were words I'll remember and cherish each day.
I'll not forget though sometimes I'm wrought
With gloom and despair and think I have nought
But loneliness and grief without my sweet son.
I must remember—I have more than just one!
No—I must not worry and I must not fret.
I must live on—the time is not yet
When God shall say, 'Let me show you the way
To a land that is fairer and brighter than day.'
Where a dear boy is waiting with a rose in his hand.
To come *skipping* to meet me in that far away land."

—Myra Foster

The loss of a child is always traumatic to moms and dads. There is a special bond built, however, between parents and a son who is as *totally* dependent on others for his care as Eddy was. The loss is particularly heart wrenching.

Was it tough on my parents? Of course it was. But as I am leafing through the pages of his memorial book, I have the luxury of viewing it from thirty-two years later. I have seen the intervening years, and I can ask the question, "Is there comfort found through the death of a loved one?" The answer is, "Yes."

Beyond weeping there is joy.

* * * * *

No heart is as vulnerable as the one going through grief. No heart requires comfort more.

The grieving process is necessary. It is perfectly understandable and normal to grieve. Not to do so would make one less than human.

Along with grief, however, there must be some comfort. Without something to cling to, the heart is overwhelmed and consumed by its grief.

The vulnerable, wounded heart may make some irrational statements. The friend trying to give comfort must realize this is their sorrow speaking. As a pastor trying to give comfort, I have heard sorrow say some things I knew the person did not believe.

What does sorrow say?

A couple facing the prospect of losing a child may say, "*I don't see how I can go on living without him.*" They just cannot picture life without him. I have heard people say this, yet life goes on.

A couple has had a loving marriage. Their lives are so intertwined with each other that the loss of the spouse causes them to say, "*I'll never be happy again.*"

A tragedy occurs; something that might have been prevented. A person may unjustly blame himself. They wonder if they couldn't have done more to prevent it. Usually, there isn't anything more that could have been done, but guilt continues to place the blame on them. Their anxiety causes them to say, "*This is more than I can bear.*"

Perhaps the most frequent thing sorrow asks is, "*Why? Why? Why?*"

How do you bring comfort to the grieving? How do you bring hope?

In the Upper Room, Jesus spoke words of comfort to the disciples. They were not idle words but were meant to bring a ray of *hope* to a very dark time.

THE SAVIOR'S COMFORT

Jesus made three general statements designed to prepare them for the coming storm.

First, he made a prediction. He said to his disciples, "*You are about to experience sorrow*. I am about to be crucified. I will die. You will think you have lost me!"

Although Jesus was making a specific prediction of his own death, it would be a fairly safe prediction to say to a person, "You are going to face grief." Sometime in a person's life, if they live a normal life span, they will lose a loved one to death.

The ray of hope he brought to them was, "*Beyond the sorrow, there will be joy.*" There was a promise made to them that their misery would not last forever, and they would laugh again.

The final statement he made was *the joy they found would never be taken away from them*. No man, circumstance, or loss could every pry it away from them.

These are three general statements he made. The specific application to the disciples centered on the resurrection of Jesus Christ.

They would suffer the pain of seeing Jesus crucified. They would mourn his death. They would sense the loss. Their feelings of guilt about how they had forsaken him and ran away would be replaced by elation. Joy would burst forth from their hearts as they proclaimed, "He is alive!"

Even persecution could not remove this joy. As Stephen is about to be stoned, we hear his exultation. "Look! The heavens are opened, and I see Jesus at the Father's right hand!"

BEYOND SORROW

How do we apply this to the person today who has been overcome by grief?

To the person who thinks they can't go on, we say, *"You will go on living."* It may not seem that way now, but life will return to some semblance of normalcy.

When I have heard someone say, "I don't see how I can live without my precious little one," I have been able to share with them the story of my brother Eddy. I have not talked about the tragedy but have been able to lovingly describe the "blessings" Eddy brought to our family in the short time we had him.

I don't know how many times someone has said afterward, "Thank you for sharing that with me. I was so distraught over losing him I did not even think about the blessing he was to my life."

Life does go on, and our lives have actually been enriched by the memories of those loved ones who have departed.

Does someone doubt they will ever be happy again? Let me reassure you, *there will be joy again.* God will not leave you to wallow in misery.

We can see an illustration of this hope in the Old Testament with the children of Israel as they wandered in the wilderness. After leaving Egypt, the Israelites became thirsty. They came to some water, but the waters were bitter and undrinkable. They named the place Marah, meaning "bitter."

When they left Marah, they came to a place called Elim or "trees." Elim was an oasis. It was a place of plenty where there was a bountiful supply of food and water. Here, the children of Israel were refreshed and enjoyed a period of rest from their wanderings.

It is like that in the path our life follows. Every life faces bitter experiences, but beyond every Marah, there is an Elim. There is a place of healing and refreshing. It is found on the trail the Lord has marked for us.

Don't get bogged down in Marah. Look toward Elim. There, the Lord has springs of refreshment to minister to your dry soul, and you will laugh again.

If you think it is more than you can bear, the Lord says *you can handle it.* He has promised not to place more on you than you are able to handle. He imparts the measure of his grace that you need, and by his strength, we stand.

Have you asked, "*Why?*" In this life, we may never understand why. Sometimes his ways are unfathomable to us. Let me set your mind at ease about something though. You have not been singled out for this treatment. Facing death is a common experience to all humans, and Christians are not exempted. We are not privileged characters who are spared all discomforts.

But the child of God *does* have a hope that extends beyond the grave.

BEYOND THIS VEIL OF TEARS

The Christian has the hope that, because of Christ, *we can see our loved ones again*. The grave is not the final parting.

Because of Jesus, there is a reunion day for the child of God. I will again see my grandfather who preached the gospel. There will be a meeting with Flossie, my grandmother, who used to pray down the fire from Heaven. One day, I'll hear a voice I have never heard before—the voice of my brother. One day, we will meet again, never to depart. And that joy man can never take away from us.

Because of that hope, we can comfort ourselves with one other fact. If our loved ones knew Jesus, they are not really dead. *They are more alive today than they ever have been.*

Early in this chapter, I made the statement, "Eddy was my brother." I should have phrased it, "Eddy *is* my brother." He still is. I haven't lost him; he is in the presence of Jesus. You can't lose someone when you know where he is.

This hope is all because of Jesus. We no longer have to fear death. Jesus has conquered it, and now death is merely a transition to a celestial city. There dwells Jesus who said, "Where I am, there you may also be." The fact is, as great as it will be to be reunited with friends and family, the reigning attraction will be him, for he is the one who made it possible. He is the one who gives comfort during the time of grief.

* * * * *

Shortly after Eddy's death, Mom was asked to teach a Sunday school class on one of the beatitudes that deals with comfort. Mom wrote it out beforehand. It states in her own words the comfort she found during that very difficult time. Since she can state it so much better than I could, I have included it in appendix II.

In the intervening years since then, I have watched my parents. I don't suppose anyone loves life more than they do.

It was tough on them, but they have a strength that goes far beyond their own. They have gone on and built a life together. They raised two sons who both became gospel preachers. In my eyes, they have had a successful life.

They are both retired now and enjoying life. If you were to ask them, I believe they would say what I have been saying in this chapter. Beyond weeping, there is joy.

As I was about to close Eddy's memorial book, I came across one more poem Mom wrote. It beautifully pictures Mom's belief that her broken rose has been mended.

Why Do You Weep, Mother?
"Why do you weep, my sweet Mother?
Why do you let the mist from your eyes
Waft gently on the earthly breeze
And drive upward to the skies?

Why is your faith so weak, my Mother?
Why do you let your sorrow increase
With each passing day since I went away?
Do you not know that I am in peace?

No longer must I lie each day,
While other children run and play.
No longer must I silent be,
While other children sing with glee.

Up here, my Mother, I sing with a band.
Up here, my Mother, I'm able to stand.

Up here, my Mother, I have no more pain.
Up here, my Mother, I'm happy again.

So—do not weep, my dear Mother,
But think of your blessed boy
Who waits each day with *dear* Jesus,
Till you shall come share his joy.

—Myra Foster

("My Eddy," "I Gave My Boy Back to Jesus Today," and "Why Do You Weep, Mother?" © 1995 by Myra Foster. Used by permission.)

The Scripture

THE SECRET OF PEACE

"Peace I leave with you, my peace I give unto you: not as the world giveth, give I unto you. Let not your heart be troubled, neither let it be afraid."

—John 14:27

"And in that day ye shall ask me nothing. Verily, verily, I say unto you, whatever ye shall ask the Father in my name, he will give it unto you. Hitherto have ye asked nothing in my name; ask and ye shall receive, that your joy may be full. These things have I spoken unto you in proverbs; but the time cometh when I shall no more speak unto you in proverbs, but I shall show you plainly of the Father. At that day ye shall ask in my name, and I say not unto you that I will pray the Father for you; For the Father himself loveth you, because ye have loved me, and have believed that I came out from God.

His disciples said unto him, Lo, now speakest thou plainly, and speakest no proverb. Now we are sure that thou knowest all things, and needest not that any man should ask thee; by this we believe that thou camest forth from God.

Jesus answered them, Do ye now believe? Behold the hour cometh, yea, is now come, that ye shall be scattered, every man to his own, and shall leave me alone; and yet I am not alone, because the Father is with me.

These things I have spoken unto you, that in me ye might have peace. In the world ye shall have tribulation: but be of good cheer; I have overcome the world."

—John 16:23–33

Chapter 14

THE SECRET OF PEACE

"I am giving you my peace. It is not like the world's peace; therefore, do not worry or fear about tomorrow."

The Lord's words perplexed Peter. The events of the past week had so troubled him that he felt as if had been caught in an approaching storm. Around him swirled all sorts of doubts, questions, and misgivings.

The events surrounding Jesus's entrance into the temple had foreshadowed the onset of the tempest. First, there was the Lord's prediction that Jerusalem would be destroyed. There on the Mount of Olives, they listened in disbelief as Jesus, with tears in his eyes, passionately bewailed the fate of the city. As troubling as that was, it was nothing compared to the scene that was to take place later in the temple.

They had wondered at the Lord's silence when he first entered the temple and looked all around at the chaos and confusion inherent in bartering. They were mystified about what was going through his mind as he walked out of the temple, sat down, and quite deliberately began fashioning a homemade whip. They were shocked with disbelief when he reentered the temple and began overturning the tables of the moneychangers, chasing them out to the tune of a cracking whip. His words ran after the fleeing traders. "My Father's house is to be a house of prayer, but you have turned it into a den of thieves!"

How would the council react to this? Peter had thought, "It's as if the Master is trying to alienate them."

If all that wasn't upsetting enough, the words Jesus was speaking as they communed around the table seemed to add to the chaos in Peter's mind. With each new "surprise" that was sprung upon them, the storm in his heart intensified.

Peter couldn't understand what the Lord was trying to get across to them. "What is he going to accomplish by telling us all these things. All it has managed to do is confuse the situation even further. And now the Lord is talking about *peace*? That's the last thing I feel right now." He hardly heard the intervening words.

Then Jesus spoke again as if to answer Peter's wondering, "I have told you all these things that you might find peace in me. There will be storms in this world, but cheer up! I have overcome the world."

Something about these words stirred a memory within Peter. His mind drifted back to a moment of crisis. The details surrounding the event were suddenly crystal clear in his mind.

The storm had blown suddenly upon them, catching them in a precarious position. Without warning, a strong wind had kicked up, followed by huge pellets of rain that would, when propelled by the wind, literally sting their faces. As fortune would have it, the disciples were right in the middle of the sea, nowhere near the coastline. And of all times for it to happen, the Lord was not with them.

As a fisherman, Peter had been on Gennesaret enough times to recognize that this was going to be a dangerous storm. He knew there was a chance their boat might not stand the tempest. Maybe it was for the best that the Master was not with them at this moment for if the boat capsized, some of them might drown.

As the wind increased, huge dark waves began rolling toward them. With the black sky and the fury of the downpour, the horizon was obliterated from their view. Their world had been reduced to the crashing of wave after wave against their boat.

Rowing became extremely difficult, and Peter could feel searing pain in his shoulders with each stroke of the oars. And now, with each wave, the ship began taking on water. The end was approaching.

Suddenly Thaddaeus exclaimed, "Look! Toward our bow! What is that?"

Peter squinted against the blowing rain and could barely make out a dark shape slowly beginning to take form through the haze of the storm. As the specter materialized in their sight, it appeared to take human form. Surely his eyes were deceiving him for it seemed to be gliding over the surface of the water, and it was coming right at them!

In the same instant, the hairs on the back of his neck stood on end, and a cold shiver swept through him. Matthew blurted out, "It's a ghost!" At those words, the entire boat went into a panic. For the first time in his life, Peter was experiencing genuine fear.

Then a voice came piercing through wind, amazingly clear and distinct considering the storm. "Don't be afraid. It's just me."

Could that be the Lord's voice? Peter still couldn't quite make him out. Peter wasn't quite sure why he responded as he did, but he found himself saying, "If that's really you Lord, you could invite me to come walking out to you on the water."

He simply said, "Come." The word seemed to draw Peter like a magnet, and before he realized it, he had stepped over the side of the boat and had taken a few steps toward him.

He was still a good distance from the Lord when he became aware of the waves slapping around his feet. He stopped, took a good look around him, and thought to himself, "What in the world am I doing out here?'

He made a sudden downward drop. Just that quickly, the water was at his knees, and his heart was in his throat. Then, as if solid ground had suddenly been jerked out from underneath his feet, he plunged into the cold water.

Peter came up coughing and sputtering. In a choking voice, he cried out with the fervent urgency of a prayer, "Lord, help me! I'm drowning!"

Instantly, Jesus was there. With one hand, he took hold of Peter's outstretched hand. Peter's gaze turned up toward the Lord. He couldn't help but focus on the Lord's eyes as he was gradually lifted out of the water.

There, in that instance, he had felt it. Gazing into his eyes, Peter had felt a calm take over him. There was still a storm raging, but he had a hold of Jesus's hand and felt at peace.

The storm had ceased when Jesus and Peter reentered the boat, but it was that moment out on the water that struck in Peter's mind.

Peter shook the memory of that moment out of his head. "What does that have to do with what's going on right now?" he thought. "Too much is happening too quickly."

How could he possibly be at peace with the tumult that was besieging him now?

* * * * *

We have set sail and found ourselves in the middle of a gale that threatened to capsize us.

We began our trip with high expectations, filled with excitement over the prospect of what lay ahead of us. Maybe your trip took the form of a new challenge, a new endeavor in life such as marriage. It could even have been a new place of service for the Lord where you give of yourself to further his kingdom. Whatever your trip, you viewed it as an adventure.

Then a storm blew up without warning. There was opposition to your efforts, and you do not understand why others don't see things as you do. Certainly your expectations were too high, and things are just not as you envisioned them. It doesn't exactly seem glamorous any longer.

Is there peace in the midst of the storm?

Jesus spoke of an unearthly peace. I call it an unearthly peace because it cannot be attained from the world. The worldly things man strives for do not bring this type of calm. When facing heartbreak, material objects bring no comfort. When opposition comes, manmade philosophies are not sufficient to ease the strain. In the time of adversity, it takes something beyond man's capabilities to be content.

Jesus lay claim to this unearthly peace. He called it *my* peace and then offered it to his disciples. He said, **"My peace I give unto you; not as the world giveth . . . Let not your heart be troubled, neither let it be afraid."** The peace that permeated the life of the Lord is at our disposal.

An examination of his life reveals someone who was always in control. Even when others took him violently to put him to death, he said, "*My* life *I* give." Yes, even at that moment, he was in control for he allowed it in order to follow the Father's will. He handled everything he faced with a supernatural calm and dignity. His was a peace that provided no room for worry and fear.

Someone is bound to be saying, "Yes, but he was the Son of God. I'm not. You would expect *him* to handle himself that way. But how can I?"

You cannot on your own. That is true, but that is why he said he would give it to us. His peace would be imparted to us.

What then is the secret of peace?

THE SECRET OF PEACE

I do not refer to it as a "secret" because it is a deeply buried gem that must be dug out. It is not hidden. In fact, it is very plain in scripture. I call it a secret because so few people avail themselves of it. It is the "obvious secret"—the diamond sitting on top of the ground that no one picks up.

The secret of peace is prayer. More specifically, it is "direct access to the Father."

Jesus gave the disciples this key in the Upper Room. He had just finished telling them that after his resurrection, their weeping would be turned to joy. Let me paraphrase the following words of Jesus found in verses 23–33:

"When you see my resurrection and feel that joy, you will no longer need to ask me to pray *for* you. You, yourselves, will be able to go directly to the Father. And if you ask him *in my name*, he will honor that request and give it unto you. In this way, your joy will be complete.

"You will be able to approach the Father because you have both loved me and trusted in me.

"I have told you these things that you might know my peace. You will have trials as long as you are in this world, but cheer up! I have overcome the world."

We have an awesome privilege as a child of his. We can walk directly into the presence of the Father. We do not need anyone to carry our petition for us. This is what Jesus was trying to get across to the disciples. This is what he said would bring them peace.

What is there about prayer that calms a storm-tossed heart? Just what are the benefits of prayer?

THE BENEFITS OF PRAYER

The benefits of prayer are both subjective and objective.

The objective benefits are those that are immeasurable. You can point them out and say, "This was a result of prayer. I specifically prayed for it, and it came to pass." On the other hand, a person might say, "I was praying for something, and the Lord showed me it was not his will. It was not in my best interest." There is a result you can easily identify: a changed mind.

The subjective benefits are not so easily defined. They are more intangible. By their very nature, there is nothing to measure them by, yet there are still very real benefits.

With that in mind, let us look first at the SUBJECTIVE BENEFITS of prayer. To do so, we must examine the very nature of prayer.

In its very basic form, *prayer is a conversation with God*. When we are confused about something, we find that we have an emotional need to talk it out with someone. Just the exercise of "getting it off our chest" will lift the weight, ease the pressure we feel, and clarify our view of things.

We experience a tremendous release just through the process of sharing our problems with someone else. Personal pressure is relieved if we feel there is a friend who understands. How much greater the relief is when the one we share it with really cares for us.

When we talk with God, we have a sympathetic ear that will listen to our every concern. Knowing we can pour our heat out to him twenty-four hours a day is a very comforting thought.

Prayer is also an act of faith. We are speaking to someone we cannot see. We can't reach out, touch a physical hand, and say "I have touched the hand of God."

We can say, however, "I have prayed and touched the heart of God." It takes faith to speak to an unseen person, and faith pleases God. When we come to God with our hurts and pain, he is not bothered by it. He delights in it and responds accordingly. There is great joy in realizing we have pleased the Father.

Prayer is an acknowledgement of our dependence on the Lord. When we come to him, we are recognizing the fact that we need help and not just anyone will do. We need his special brand of help.

Acknowledging our dependence on him prepares our heart for his response. By realizing our insufficiency, we open our heart and are more susceptible to his guidance.

Prayer is not the last resort. *It is a positive step.* When we pray, we are showing our confidence in the one we petition. We are demonstrating our firm belief that he is able and willing to aid us. We should never say, "When all else fails, pray." It should be our natural inclination. And it should be much more than just our response when we are in trouble. It ought to be a daily habit.

Now that we have glimpsed the nature of prayer, let's examine the OBJECTIVE BENEFITS of prayer.

The first benefit could be considered either objective or subjective. When we pray, *the Holy Spirit meets with us and ministers to us.* Even though the Spirit is unseen, the results of his ministry to us are observable.

When he wraps his loving arms around us, his peace envelops us. There is a change in our demeanor. The stress in our countenance is replaced by a calm visage. Even our actions will be changed from "the outburst of the uptight" to "the response of the at peace." It will be noticeable to all those around us.

All of these benefits we have talked about should be enough to cause us to pray regularly, but they all pale when compared with this next one. *The Father honors the prayer made in the name of Jesus.*

Praying in the name of Jesus means more than just tacking the words "in Jesus's name" onto the end of our prayer. It first denotes that we belong to him. As a possession of his, we have no merit of our own to approach the Father. But since we have been purchased by the blood of Jesus, we invoke his name, and the Father takes note of it.

Praying in his name also indicates our *submission* to him or our willingness to yield to his will. We are never to pray selfishly for our own desires but are to pray in God's will. Do not think that a person can fail to be in submission to him and still get all he asks for. It doesn't matter how many times you say the words "in Jesus's name" during your prayer. If you are not yielded to him in total submission, you are not praying in his name.

When we pray in the right attitude, however, and invoke the Son's name, it catches the Father's attention. The Father always honors the Son. If we belong to him and are submitted to him, the Father will respond when we invoke that precious name.

Through his name, we have access to the Father.

Through his name, we have the attention of the Father.

Through his name, we touch the heart of the Father.

Through his name, we have our petition.

And through his name, there is an abundance of peace.

Touching the heart of the Father brings a quick and sure response from God. Even as Peter cried out in distress on the Sea of Galilee, we have the privilege to call upon him. And just as Peter received help in his time of need, we will see his hand stretched out toward us. When we touch his heart, we touch his hand as he lifts us out of our predicament.

At the touch of his helping hand, peace permeates our soul, reaching to every corner or distant edifice of our heart. Wherever stress may reside, supernatural peace seeks it out and banishes it.

Let me stop right here and ask a question. What would have happened on the Sea of Galilee if Peter had not have cried out to Jesus? He might have drowned, or he might have even survived it. It might have been possible for him to swim back to the boat and be pulled in by the other disciples.

But how would he have felt inside? There would have been no peace. He would always be disturbed by the fact that he had stepped out and failed.

Prayer is not just the secret to deliverance. It is the secret to peace of mind.

Does other scripture bear this out? Yes, it does. We can read in Philippians 4:1–8 where the Apostle Paul addresses it in much more detail adding more insight into the peace of God. I will not cover that scripture here, but I have included a few comments about it in appendix III.

Jesus promised an unearthly peace to us, his followers. He said it came from him, and the key to unlocking it was to ask of the Father.

In the middle of this promise, he recognized there would be trials and even predicted the disciples' failure.

But because he was facing the storm for us, he could say the following words:

> **"These things I have spoken unto you, that in me ye might have peace. In the world ye shall have tribulation: but be of good cheer; I have overcome the world."**
>
> —John 16:33

The Scripture

JESUS HAS PRAYED FOR YOU

"These words spoke Jesus, and lifted up his eyes to heaven, and said, Father, the hour is come; glorify thy Son, that thy Son also may glorify thee."

—John 17:1

"Now they have known that all things, whatsoever thou hast given me, are of thee. For I have given unto them the words which thou gavest me; and they have received them, and have known surely that I came out from thee, and they have believed that thou didst send me.

I pray for them; I pray not for the world, but for them whom thou hast given me; for they are thine."

—John 17:7–9

"And now I am no more in the world, but these are in the world, and I come to thee. Holy Father, keep through thine own name those whom thou hast given me, that they may be one, as we are.

While I was with them in the world, I kept them in thy name; those that thou gavest me I have kept, and none of them is lost, but the son of perdition, that the scripture might be fulfilled.

And now come I to thee; and these things I speak in the world, that they might have my joy fulfilled in themselves.

I have given them thy word; and the world hath hated them, because they are not of the world, even as I am not of the world. I pray not that thou shouldest take them out of the world, but that thou shouldest keep them from the evil. They are not of the world, even as I am not of the world.

Sanctify them through thy truth; thy word is truth."

—John 17:11–17

"Neither pray I for these alone, but for them also who shall believe on me through their word; That they all may be as one, as thou Father, art in me, and I in thee, that they also may be one in us; that the world may believe that thou hast sent me."

—John 17:20–21

Chapter *15*

JESUS HAS PRAYED FOR YOU

Our little group was led into the room. Its rock walls were cold to the touch and gave the enclosure more of a cavelike feeling than of anything else. In my mind's eye, I tried to imagine what it would have been like to be kept in this holding cell. Even if for only a very short time, the dampness and the darkness must have made it a very lonely place.

Then our guide directed our attention toward one of the walls. There, very visibly, was a section that was much darker than the rest of the rock. The darkened rock took on the resemblance of a man on his knees with his arms raised in a traditional Hebrew position of prayer. The shadowlike feature of the image gave the room a certain haunting quality. You could almost feel the anguish of a man making supplication to God as he awaited trial.

In 1973, I was privileged to visit the Holy Land. It was a marvelous trip that I enjoyed immensely. We spent eight days crisscrossing Israel and then spent two days in Rome, Italy. To be perfectly honest, I became so enthralled with Jerusalem that I could have spent the entire time there. I became fascinated with the archaeology of Jerusalem.

All round Jerusalem, there are many "traditional" sites that are associated with different stories from one of the Gospels. Some have a certain authenticity such as the pavement beneath the Fortress Antonia where the soldiers of Pilate played the "king's game" with their prisoners. Some sites have little more than tradition to support them and may have been preserved strictly for the booming tourist trade.

Whereas the old city of Jerusalem is little changed in atmosphere from the way things were in the time of Christ, the actual street level of that time is several feet below the present street level. This presents a question in your mind as you walk the Via Dolorosa and observe the different Stations of the Cross. If the present street level is elevated above the level of the time of Christ, how does tradition know where Christ stumbled under the cross?

Another consideration that makes verification difficult is the fact that whenever Jerusalem has been destroyed, which it has been many times, the people would rebuild it using the same blocks and stones from the previous buildings. When we were taken to the traditional site of the Upper Room, this caused me to wonder, "How do they know this is the actual site?" Once again, it is tradition.

Then there is the controversy over which of two sites is the actual location of Golgotha. Is it the hill underneath the Church of the Holy Sepulcher, or is it Gordon's Calvary located north of the city walls? A case can be made for both sites.

For me, none of these questions diminish the trip at all or lessen the spiritual experience of walking the land Jesus walked. If anything, they make the study of Jerusalem much more interesting to me. It is like the fascination of a mystery. What clues can point to the actual site?

There are some sites that, for all practical purposes, are absolutely certain. There are the Mount of Olives and the Garden of Gethsemane. There is the general area of the Temple Mount. As mentioned before, there is the Fortress Antonia where, in all likelihood, Jesus was abused, whipped, and brought to trial before Pilate.

Perhaps the most certain site from an archaeological standpoint of all the sites in Jerusalem is the excavation of the ruins of the House of Caiaphas, the high priest.

While we were there, we saw the excavated pathway running from Gethsemane to Caiaphas's house. Gazing upon it, we knew that almost assuredly, Jesus was led over these stones to his appointment with Caiaphas after his arrest in the garden.

We sat in the outer courtyard where Peter warmed himself with the enemies of Jesus and listened as our host related the biblical story of Peter's denial of the Lord. We could almost feel the cool night air, the crackling fire, and the fear and uncertainty Peter must have experienced that night.

Then we were led down to the holding cell where Jesus was probably kept during the short time between his appearance before the high priest and his appearance before Pilate. As we looked at the "shadow" on the wall, our guide remarked, "Tradition holds that this shadow appeared as Jesus was praying to the Father on that night."

In the middle of archaeological certainty, tradition had once again raised its head. There was no addressing of how or even why his image should be transferred to the wall. It was merely stated that it was tradition. Perhaps people wanted to believe that as a reminder of the importance Jesus placed upon prayer.

Whether or not his prayer left its mark on that wall is questionable at best. But there is a prayer of his that left its mark *on my life*. It is his high priestly prayer as recorded in John chapter 17.

A truth is tucked away in this prayer. From the day I learned this truth, it has been a source of blessing, encouragement, and motivation in my Christian walk.

This truth has marked my life.

* * * * *

Jesus's life was characterized as a life of prayer. Everything he did was bathed in prayer.

His prayers left its mark on all who came in contact with him. We see the imprint of his prayers in the miracles he did. We can follow the trace of his prayers in the lives he touched.

The scripture itself bears the stamp of his prayer life.

Mark 1:35 records that Jesus rose early in the morning, retreated to a solitary place, and prayed.

Luke 3:21 asserts that at his baptism, Jesus prayed and then the heavens were opened.

Luke 6:12 states that he went up into a mountain and prayed all night.

On the Mount of Transfiguration, as related in Luke chapter 9, it was while he prayed that his countenance was altered, and he was transfigured before Peter, James, and John.

His prayers made quite an impression upon the disciples. So much so that they asked him to teach them to pray. That is when he gave them the model prayer that is known as the Lord's Prayer.

We can make note of the fervor and earnestness in his prayer as we read his prayer in the Garden of Gethsemane. There, as he submitted to his Father, his agony was so great that his sweat became as drops of blood.

His heart is exposed in Luke 22:31–32. There he told Peter that Satan wanted to defeat him but then added, **"I have prayed for thee, that thy faith fail not."**

His entire life was saturated in prayer. Is it any wonder that in the Upper Room his thoughts turned to prayer?

JESUS'S HIGH PRIESTLY PRAYER

He had spoken his final words of encouragement. He had said what was on his heart. Now his gaze moved from one disciple to another. Each one of these eleven men (Judas having already left to betray him) stirred a deep compassion within the heart of Jesus.

The storm clouds were gathering near. They were about to break upon them with a fury like they had never known.

There was silence around the room for a few moments as Jesus stored the image of these men in his heart. Then his eyes lifted up to Heaven, and in a voice filled with passion, he began to pray.

This is the perfect example of intercessory prayer. He had just finished telling them they would have the authority to enter God's throne room in prayer for themselves, and they would not need to go through another. Yet he sensed the need to intercede to the Father on their behalf. He would not fail to pray for them by saying, "Let them pray for themselves." Interceding for them was a ministry he would not shirk.

Jesus was the perfect intercessor for *he was willing to take their place*. I believe the true intercessor that touches the heart of God has the willingness to suffer for the one he prays for. I can think of two other men in scripture who demonstrated this same willingness.

Moses interceded for the children of Israel in Exodus 32:31–32. He acknowledged the people's sin but asked God to forgive them. He then expressed the intercessor's willingness by saying, "But if not, blot my name out of thy book also." God's response was to tell Moses it was his prerogative whom he would blot out, and the people would suffer the natural consequence for their sin. But his hand was stayed from wiping them off the face of the earth.

Paul expressed this willingness in Romans 9:3. While under a heavy burden for Israel, he said, "If it were possible, I would wish myself accursed from God (in Hell) if it meant that Israel could be saved." It was not a possible transaction to trade his salvation for all of Israel's, but that willingness displayed the intercessory nature of Paul's heart.

This type of holy compassion touches the Lord's heart, and while transference of suffering may not take place, his hand can be moved to relieve the pain and comfort the one in need. This is intercessory prayer after the heart of God.

As wonderful as these human examples are, Jesus alone becomes the complete, ultimate intercessor. Even while he is praying in the Upper Room, Judas is conspiring to betray the Lord. The forces are coming together to arrest Jesus. Not only will Jesus demonstrate a willingness to take mankind's place, but he will literally suffer in their stead. In this way, Jesus stands alone. Only he could have taken upon himself the sin of the world and died in our place.

Because of his willingness and ability to take our suffering, he becomes the genuine intercessory, and his prayer becomes the authentic example of intercessory prayer.

"THE HOUR IS COME"

Jesus began to pray, "Father, the crucial time is here. I ask that you glorify me so that I will be able to glorify you."

The stream of Jesus's holy life had run into the raging torrent of human rebellion and had merged at the confluence of God's will. It was the critical moment in human history.

All his life, Jesus had been facing this moment. He had glorified the Father by giving the disciples the Father's word. He had pointed out the path that leads to eternal life when he said, **"And this is life eternal, that they might know thee the only true God, and Jesus Christ, whom Thou hast sent"** (verse 3). Now, the very words he prayed gave this specific hour the essence of some momentous crossroads of humanity.

What was so crucial about "this hour?" What made it so critical?

First, *he was about to make the final sacrifice* and thus fulfill the law. He had pointed toward eternal life, but now he was about to actually make the provision for it. At stake was the salvation of all who would believe. Without the perfect sacrifice, man could not come to know the only true God. The hour of his offering had come.

Secondly, *it was the hour when the storm would break upon the disciples.* Three years of teaching, training, and preparing these men had culminated this past week. Now things would happen that they would not immediately understand. The preparation was over. The hour of their trial had come.

But not only that, *it was the hour when Jesus's submission to the Father would be tested.* As one who was equal to the Father, in fact one with him, he did not have to choose this course. Yet in order to redeem man, he would submit himself to the Father's will. The storm of submission would break upon Jesus in Gethsemane.

In consideration of this dark hour, Jesus first prayed for himself. He prayed that he would glorify the Father and, in faith, looked beyond the horror of that death to the resurrection and ascension when he would be restored to his preincarnate glory (verse 5).

But then his thoughts turned to his disciples.

"I PRAY FOR THEM"

Jesus had been very diligent during his time with the disciples to provide them with all that they would need to do the task set before them. For three years, he had been equipping and preparing them for the moment he would leave them. It was with loving care he had supplied all their needs.

How had he prepared them? Verses 7–8 gives two essentials to their equipping. *He gave them a word from God* and then *the disciples received it*. Both are essential to spiritual growth. To be strengthened in the Lord, we must hear a word from God, and we must receive it even if it is uncomfortable.

The disciples were totally dependent upon Jesus's presence. That was their comfort zone. But soon, he would be taken away. Their area of comfort would be removed. They would not have his bodily presence with them. Jesus felt a strong urge and a need to lift them up in prayer.

He made four specific requests on behalf of the disciples.

He first prayed *for their unity*.

His prayer was, "**Keep through thine own name those whom thou hast given me, that they may be one, as we are.**"

In a few short hours, they would be scattered. Their fear would drive them in different directions. If they were to weather the storm and do the task they were called to do, they would require each other's help. They desperately needed that strong bond that comes by being related.

He also prayed that *their joy would be complete*.

Verse 13 records that he was praying for them **that they might have my joy fulfilled in themselves.**

We have already covered in chapter 10 how we can have joy. We saw there that joy is dependent upon our relationship with the vine, abiding in Christ, bearing fruit, remaining pure, and continuing in his love.

The only thing that remains to be pointed out here is Jesus WANTS his disciples to have joy. It is not his desire that his followers be sad and forlorn. He specifically prayed that this group of men would experience his joy.

He next prayed for *their protection from the world.*

"I pray not," He said, **"that thou shouldest take them out of the world, but that thou shouldest keep them from the evil."**

He did not pray for one thing. He did not pray for them to be removed from the world. It was not God's desire to separate them from all contact with the world. The practice of going to a monastery, severing all earthly contacts in order to become more holy, and associating only with other believers is not God's design.

If the church were to isolate itself from the world, who would witness to God's saving grace? Who would be light and salt to a troubled world?

Whereas few Christians would desire to go to a monastery, I have heard many Christians express this desire: "I wish I could work in a Christian company. Wouldn't it be great if all those I worked with were Christians?" This is little more than the same desire to be isolated from the world.

Did you ever stop to consider that perhaps God placed you in that work situation to be a shining light for him? Instead of looking for a total Christian environment, we should be asking, "Lord, how may I serve you where I am?"

We are not *of* the world, but we are *in* the world. Jesus's prayer for the disciples was not to remove them but that while they were in the world, they would be protected from the evil of the world.

Lastly, he prayed *they would be set apart and sent to bear witness.*

Verses 17–18 record his words to the Father: **"Sanctify them** (set them apart) **through thy truth: thy word is truth. As thou hast sent me into the world, even so have I also sent them into the world."**

They were to be set apart, to be different for a purpose. That purpose was to spread the gospel to the far reaches of the world. That was their commission.

Someone may be reading all this and saying, "So that is his prayer for the disciples. Big deal! What does that mean to me?"

Hang on to your hats! There is a truth coming up that has been a source of blessing and challenge to me since the day I read it.

THE SUBLIME TRUTH

Jesus Has Prayed for You

When Jesus finished praying for his disciples, this is the prayer that the Word of God records in verse 20:

"Neither pray I for these alone, but for THEM ALSO WHICH SHALL BELIEVE ON ME THROUGH THEIR WORD."

Jesus prayed for all those who would believe on him through the words the disciples spoke. That means *Jesus prayed for me!*

I believed after I heard the Word of God preached. That Word was inspired by the Holy Spirit but penned by the hands of the apostles. I was included in that prayer, and if you have believed on him, so were you. The same thing he desired for the disciples he desires for us.

There have been many times when I was feeling down that someone dropped me a note to tell me they had prayed for me. Those notes served to lift me up. Just the thought that someone cared enough to pray for me was a real blessing.

Can you remember a time when someone shared with you that they were praying for you? Did it prove to be an encouragement to you?

Now think on this. Jesus *himself* left you a note in John 17:20 saying he has prayed for you. If hearing that from another Christian can encourage you, then consider this. The Son of God himself has prayed for us, and it was the same prayer he prayed for the disciples.

Have you ever been discouraged? Have you felt depression consuming your life? Has the trial you are facing sapped you of your strength? Remember, JESUS HAS PRAYED THAT YOUR JOY WOULD BE COMPLETE.

Has temptation ever stared you in the face? You have tried to do right, but in a moment of exhaustion, when your guard is down, it presents itself. It seems so attractive, and you don't think you are strong enough to resist. Think on this: JESUS HAS PRAYED THAT YOU WOULD BE KEPT FROM EVIL.

Have you been involved in his service and feel like you have not accomplished anything? JESUS HAS PRAYED FOR YOUR MINISTRY.

Has there been friction between you and another Christian? Has it become a source of distress in your life? The blessed truth is JESUS HAS PRAYED FOR OUR UNITY.

Are you facing the trial of your life?
JESUS HAS PRAYED FOR YOU.

Standing in that holding cell at the house of Caiaphas, being reminded that Jesus prayed was a blessing indeed. But thinking back on it, I am reminded of another prayer of his.

It was his high priestly prayer.
It left its mark in God's word.
It left its mark on my life.
It tells me Jesus cares for me.
It tells me Jesus prayed for me.

Chapter 16

RISING ABOVE THE CARES

The streets were crowded to the point where you could hardly make your way. People jostled each other, each going about his or her own special business, for in a little over a day, all Israel would observe its greatest national day of remembrance: the Passover. On one side, two men were engaged in the lively art of barter, each enjoying the game almost as much as the deal. On the other, two children were pushing their way through the crowd on their way to some secret rendezvous where they might be engaged in whatever play game would strike their fancy. All around were the sights, sounds, and smells of the impending celebration. The noise was such that you could barely carry on an intelligent conversation.

All the noise, hustle, and bustle brought back many memories to John of past Passover seasons. He loved this time of year and wanted to soak in as much of the atmosphere as he could. He had to confess, however, that the hassle of the crowd was an annoyance to him. To him, it seemed to be a distraction from what Passover was all about.

As the disciples approached the household where the supper had been prepared, John couldn't help but notice the tired blank stares on some of the faces they were passing. It dawned on him as he looked on his compatriots that they were reflecting the same weariness in their own countenances. The events and disturbances of the last few days were really taking a toll on them.

John could tell this was going to be an unusual supper. Earlier, Jesus had sent Peter and himself with some specific instructions on how to prepare for it. They had found the large, upper room as Jesus had said and began to make ready. What would make this supper unusual was they were celebrating the Passover early, not on the normal day.

Another glaring oddity was the fact that there was no Passover lamb at the meal. Perhaps, John thought, this was something special Jesus was doing. Maybe they would have another Passover supper where a lamb would be provided.

As they entered the household, the owner greeted them. "Welcome, Master," he said as he embraced the Lord. "Everything is ready as you asked." He then ushered them to the stairs leading up to the room. The disciples slowly began their ascent to the Upper Room.

As they moved up the steps, the sounds from the street outside became fainter and fainter. What had been an overwhelming, chaotic symphony of sounds was now a slight hum in the background. As they filed in and gathered around the table, the door was shut, further muffling the sound.

As each event unfolded throughout the evening, John began pondering the words Jesus was speaking. It was obvious to John from the painful expressions on their faces that the other disciples were extremely disturbed by all that was transpiring. John was confused also, but the more he thought about those riveting words, the calm they seemed to produce. He still did not understand, but there was just something about his words.

"Tomorrow might be a difficult day," he thought. Jesus had indicated that it would be. "But tonight, let me just soak up his words and enjoy his presence. I will need some strength to face whatever comes."

His attention was drawn once again to the muffled sounds below. Out there in the real world, there were probably two people in a heated argument. Somewhere out there, a child was crying. Out there was a world of stress, tension, and confusion. It would not be long till he would reenter that chaotic scene.

"But for right now," he thought, "I don't want to think about all that." Whatever was going on out there in the street, whatever he would have to face, let it happen.

Tonight, he was spending time with Jesus.

* * * * *

Coming out of the Upper Room, John faced the same trial the rest of the disciples faced. Initially, he was scattered along with the others, but throughout the entire ordeal, we find John in Caiaphas's house while Jesus is being examined for it was him who came out and spoke to the door keeper to let Peter in. John is the only disciple who we have a record of actually being at the crucifixion. He seems to be the only one who wanted to stay close to the Lord during his passion.

Clearly, the words Jesus spoke in the Upper room had an impact on John. His account of the Upper Room experience focuses more on the words Jesus spoke than on the events that took place. In fact, John does not even mention the instituting of the Lord's Supper, which would later become an ordinance of the church. But *the words* Jesus spoke there take up five chapters of scripture.

If I may speculate a little, perhaps it was the strength he received from those words that caused him to follow close to the Lord during the trial.

How do you handle a harried world filled with stress? How can you rise above the cares of the world? To get right to the point, you rise above the cares by figuratively going to an upper room. At that place, you meet Jesus and spend time communing with him.

Your own personal upper room may be a "prayer closet," a study, or merely a place within your heart. Wherever that "place" is, it is where you meet with God. It is where you bring all your pain, fear, and trepidation. It is where you seek for answers. There you find direction. There you gain strength. There your sadness is turned to joy.

Having an upper room is essential to the spiritual and emotional well-being of a child of God. Only there can we keep things in perspective. Only there, as we enter into that sanctuary, can we understand the trial of our life.

When we enter into that holy haven, we will make a discovery. This discovery is illustrated by a detail that John leaves out. We will need to go to Luke's writings to find it.

> **"And he sent Peter and John saying, Go and prepare us the Passover, that we may eat.**
>
> **And he shall show you a large upper room furnished: there make ready."**
>
> —Luke 22:8, 12

When Peter and John entered the house Jesus had directed them to, they were ushered into a large upper room. There they found that the room *was already furnished*. Everything they would need to prepare for the Passover was already there. They needed to bring nothing with them. They were provided with all that they would need.

When we enter our own personal upper room, we make the same discovery. The room is furnished. All we need as we face the cares of the world is found right there. What we find there prepares us for life. What we gain in personal communion with the Lord is sufficient for our time of testing. *Jesus is all-sufficient.*

It may sound strange for a preacher to admit this, but I do not have all the answers. There are some problems people bring to me that leave me feeling inadequate to help. BUT I DO KNOW WHERE THE ANSWER CAN BE FOUND! I know the one who has all the answers. The answer to whatever problem you may face is found in your upper room, speaking with the Wonderful Counselor.

Has a traumatic event gripped your life? Are you facing the trial of your life? Perhaps a multitude of worldly cares, scores of minor annoyances, have ganged up on you to make life miserable. How do you cope?

Rise above the cares of this life. Go to an upper room. Spend some time with Jesus.

We have sailed through the storm. We have come out the other side of it and can look back upon it. While we were in the middle of our trial, it seemed desperate. We could see no way out. We didn't see how we could stand, but here we are. We now have the advantage of hindsight.

Not only am I speaking form a scriptural view point, but I am also speaking from experience. Like everyone else, I have been through difficult times. I can tell you there are some lessons I learned by going through the trial. What are the lessons we learn in the dark times?

The first lesson we learn is *the trial is of short duration.* It only appears as if it will go on forever. If it seems like there is no end in sight, take heart in this notion. The trial will end. It will all pass. Beyond the darkness, there is the shining light of God's love. He will not keep you in that particular trial.

The next lesson we are taught is *Jesus is very near to us during our trial.* Some of the most precious times I have experienced with the Lord came during times of testing. During these times, he would visit with me while I was reading his word, and it was as if he was trying to say to me, "I love you. Don't give up."

But to be perfectly honest with you, there were times I wondered where he was. I couldn't sense his presence. It was only in retrospection sometime later that I could see his hand at work. I couldn't see what he was doing at the time, but all the while, he was doing a valuable work in my life. Even when I wasn't aware of him, he was still present and active on my behalf.

Remember that while the disciples were grieving over the death of Jesus, they could not see that it was setting up the resurrection. A realization I have come to after passing through various trials is *the person I have become is a product of all those trials.*

Not long ago, during a time of self-evaluation, something became very clear to me. Any spiritual insight I might have was developed during a time of testing. If I have any strength to stand, I gained it by actually facing a strong wind. If there are any character traits in me that are admirable, they matured in the fire.

I can look back and say those trials are a part of me. God used them to make me what I am, and I thank God for the trials. If they can make me more like Jesus, then praise his holy name.

Perhaps the most blessed truth I have learned from it all is *it is possible to have peace and joy throughout the trial.* I do not have to be totally dejected or depressed. Like the Christians at Thessalonica, I can go through affliction with joy.

That does not necessarily mean I like the bad things that happen to me, but it does mean I can rejoice in the Lord. I can rejoice over what he is doing in my life and over what the eventual outcome will be. I can rejoice in that he counted me worthy to bear it all. And I can rejoice in the heightened sense of awareness concerning his presence.

But most of all, I can still rejoice that I have *him.* There's no reason to be so engrossed in my problems that I forget the blessing he has bestowed upon me.

Maybe you're not there yet. Maybe you're still engulfed by raging waters, and these lessons haven't become evident to you. Let me make a suggestion. Take the words Jesus spoke in the Upper Room to your own private upper room. Let *his* words of life minister to you and give you the comfort and strength you need as you face your trial.

Perhaps you feel you have already failed the test. Your storm came, and you went under. You wonder what you can do with a life already messed up. Keep one fact in mind. Initially, the disciples failed the test. They ran for their lives in the garden. Peter even denied the Lord. They failed miserably. They did not stand true.

But praise the Lord we serve the God of second chances. They found forgiveness and came back stronger than they were before. They then proceeded to turn the world upside down for Jesus.

There is no hopeless case. In whatever condition we may be, we can rest and trust in the Lord Jesus who walks with us over the stormy sea of our trial.

"Oh, bless our God, you peoples!
And make the voice of his praise to be heard,
Who keeps our soul among the living,
And does not allow our feet to be moved.
For you, O God, have proved us;
You have refined us as silver is refined.
You brought us into the net;
You laid affliction on our backs.
You have caused men to ride over our heads;
We went through the fire and through water;
But you brought us out to rich fulfillment."

—Psalm 66:8–12 (NKJV)

The End

Appendix 7

THE GIFT OF THE HOLY SPIRIT
HIS OPERATION IN OUR LIVES

1.   HE IS OUR GUARANTEE.

> **"Now he that hath wrought us for the selfsame thing is God, who hath given unto us the earnest of the Spirit."**
>
> —Second Corinthians 5:5

Whenever someone is contemplating making a large purchase and they want the seller to hold the object for them so that no one else will claim it, they will give the seller what is called "earnest money." This is a payment that will guarantee that the seller will hold it, and it is the promise that the buyer will actually buy the object. If for some reason the buyer does not purchase the item, he forfeits the earnest money.

In the verses prior to this verse, the Apostle Paul had been speaking of the future glorified body that we will be clothed with. When this frail body is laid aside, there is a heavenly, eternal body we will inherent. He goes on to say the believer has an earnest desire, and we groan to attain that state. We long to be in God's presence, clothed in immortality.

The beginning of this verse states it is God himself who has placed that desire in the hearts of his children. Along with this desire, he has given us a guarantee that he will perform it. He has given unto us the gift of the Holy Spirit. Just like earnest money, he is the guarantee that God will redeem our physical bodies at the resurrection. The Spirit is the earnest money of our redemption. We know we will be physically, bodily raised because we have the guarantee of the Holy Spirit dwelling within us.

Our redemption is secure. We have the "earnest."

2.   HE SEALS US.

"That we should be to the praise of his glory, who first trusted in Christ. In whom ye also trusted, after that ye heard the word of truth, the gospel of your salvation: in whom also after that ye believed, ye were sealed with that Holy Spirit of promise."

—Ephesians 1:12–13

In the ancient world, when the reigning king or potentate passed a decree, he would place his seal upon it. He would do so by impressing his ring in clay on the document. This validated the document, and without a seal, no document was considered authentic. Sometimes the document was closed up by the seal, and no one but the authorized party could break the king's seal.

The signet ring used to seal the document represented the king's authority. It carried with it the power of his dominion.

The scripture says we are **sealed with the Holy Spirit of promise.** The Holy Spirit is what seals our salvation. Having this seal signifies three things.

First, it indicates our salvation is *validated* by the presence of the Holy Spirit. The imparting of the Holy Spirit at the moment of conversion gives authenticity to the work of regeneration. After this indwelling, the subsequent working of the Holy Spirit in and through our lives, producing an undeniable change in our behavior, gives abundant evidence of what has transpired within us. Romans 8:16 and First John3:24 also indicate we can find great assurance of our salvation by the presence of the Holy Spirit.

Secondly, our salvation is *secured* by the Holy Spirit. As the author and finisher of our faith, Jesus Christ places the seal of the Holy Spirit upon the believer. No one can break that seal save the one in authority, and the scripture is replete with passages that says he will *never* leave us and *nothing* can separate us from his love. If he WILL NOT break the seal, NOTHING ELSE CAN. We are secure.

Lastly, this rests upon the *authority* of the king himself. All the power and omnipotence of the King of kings and Lord of lords holds this seal in place. With regal authority and unlimited ability, he holds the believer in his hand and places his stamp of approval and owner-ship upon his child.

3. HE IS OUR TEACHER.

"Howbeit when he, the Spirit of truth, is come, he will guide you into all truth."

—John 16:13a

Skeptics have long questioned whether the words or events in the Gospel accounts were dependable, or if the disciples' faulty mem-ory and wishful thinking gave rise to certain "legends" and "myths" concerning the Lord. There is one word to describe this mindset. That word is UNBELIEF. The people who espouse this doctrine are unbelievers and *do not possess* the Spirit of truth that guides believers in their understanding of the truths of God's word.

It was not strictly the disciples' memories that brought the Gospels together. In John 14:26, Jesus told his disciples that the Spirit would **"bring all things to your remembrance, whatever I have said unto you."** As these men preached and later penned the words of the Lord, it was the Spirit that brought the words to their memories and preserved them from error. The Gospels are accurate and dependable because of the Teacher, the Holy Spirit, that brought them to mind.

It was the Holy Spirit that instructed Paul for three years of solitude in Arabia (Gal. 1:17) in order to clarify and codify the doctrine of Grace.

It is the Holy Ghost that instructs us today in truth and unlocks the mysteries of God's Word. Some claim the Bible is too difficult to understand when, actually, it is very plain. They overlook the fact that we have been given a teacher to guide us in our understanding of the Word. He brings things to our understanding.

4.   HE IS OUR GUIDE.

"For as many as are led by the Spirit of God, they are the sons of God."

—Romans 8:14

Man, on his own, can really make a mess of things. All one has to do is take a look at our world today to see this perfectly illustrated. Crime is rampant. It seems like more and more we are hearing of tragedies that reflect unnatural tendencies or actions that are just plain sick. We hear of rape, child abuse, incest, and the murder of innocent bystanders, and we wonder what in the world is going on. A look at the actions of nations shows no improvement in man's warped thinking. Just when it seems there might be peace, war breaks out somewhere in the world.

In man's fallen condition, he cannot successfully order his steps.

Even Christians with a desire to do right will, if left to their own devices, make horrible mistakes in judgment. We need a guide to know how to live and what decisions are wise. It must be someone who knows what all the ramifications of our actions will be and can see all the hidden pitfalls we cannot see. The Holy Spirit is that guide who orders our steps.

However, to ignore him in the decision-making process places us in the position of doing it on our own as if we had no guide. To avail ourselves of his leadership requires *yielding control* of our lives to him. Learning how to yield to him is developed in the process of spiritual growth and necessitates a *desire* to follow his direction.

"The steps of a good man are ordered by the Lord: and he delighteth in his way" (Ps. 37:23).

Praise God for the wonderful leadership of our guide, companion, and friend, the Holy Spirit. Let us never take for granted his wisdom.

5.   HE GIVES ASSURANCE.

"The Spirit itself beareth witness with our spirit, that we are the children of God."

—Romans 8:16

We have alluded to this fact before, but it bears repeating. We find great assurance of our salvation by the presence of the Holy Spirit in our lives.

Let me illustrate it this way: you cannot convince me someone could move into my home without me being aware he was living there. I would find some dirty dishes and say "I don't remember dirtying these." I would come across some clothes and think, "These are not my clothes. Where did they come from?" Even if the absurd notion of someone moving into my house without my knowledge were possible and even if I never actually saw him coming in and out of my house, *there would be some evidence he was there.*

The Scripture teaches that the Holy Spirit indwells believers. In fact, First Corinthians 6:19 teaches that our body is the temple of the Holy Spirit. At conversion, the Spirit comes to live within the believer. Do you really believe God could take up residence in your life without your being aware of it? You may not always see how he is working within you, but there will be some evidence he is there.

When I see myself responding to opposition with a calm and graciousness that is clearly not my own, that is evidence of someone within. When I have power and boldness beyond my abilities, that is ample proof.

6. HE GIVES POWER TO WITNESS.

"But ye shall receive power, after that the Holy Ghost is come upon you: and ye shall be witnesses unto me both in Jerusalem, and in all Judea, and in Samaria, and unto the uttermost part of the earth."

—Acts 1:8

Sometimes it seems as if the viewpoint of some Christians is the Holy Spirit has come into their lives for the sole purpose of making them "feel good." They might not actually say that, but they want to come to church, have a good time, rejoice, get caught up in ecstasy, and perhaps be entertained without making a commitment to actively serve the Lord Jesus Christ. There is never a thought of actually sharing their faith with a hurting soul. Even though they would never phrase it in that manner, that is what their actions say over and over again.

These Christians need to take a close look at this passage of scripture. This verse tells us three things of the Spirit's impact on the Christian.

First, it says *it is the Christian's responsibility to spread the Gospel.* They were to take the witness as they went. We are not to sit on our blessed assurance and serve ourselves. God requires us to spread the gospel, and he even gives us a plan to carry it out. What is outlined in this verse is God's plan for evangelizing, beginning at home and spreading to the entire world.

The next thing it says is *we need the Spirit to witness effectively.* The Spirit serves to bring power, authority, and boldness to the witness of Christians.

But it is the third thing that is the most amazing. When the Holy Spirit would come upon them, they were not asked to be a witness. It was stated as a fact, YOU WILL BE WITNESSES. This makes it clear that witnessing is not a suggestion. It more than just a command. *Boldly witnessing is actually a byproduct of the Holy Spirit.* There seems to be no question that the person filled with the Holy

Spirit will witness. It is the natural result of being controlled by the Spirit of God.

Therefore, our responsibility, the overwhelming need of the lost world, and the very nature of the Holy Spirit requires the Christian to be a witness to the saving grace of our Lord Jesus Christ.

Appendix 11

(Shortly after my brother Eddy died, my mom was asked to speak to their Sunday school class on the following beatitude. Since she can better describe her feelings than I ever could, I have included her lesson here in the hope it will be a comfort to someone.)

"Blessed are they that mourn, for they shall be comforted."

—Matthew 5:45

When I first learned of the beatitude that Junior had given me to talk about, my first reaction was, "No, I can't do it. Why does Junior want to do this to me? Why give me this one? Why not another one?" But the more I thought about it, I knew Junior was right. One who has experienced death recently in his immediate family would be the logical one to talk about this particular beatitude. They should be able to voice their opinion as to the truth in this verse, "Blessed are they that mourn for they shall be comforted."

I have always been very emotional about anything that concerns my family. Half the time, I can't even talk to Jobo about some little incident without crying. I know I cannot stand before you as a class and *tell* what is on my heart, and I do have so much to say. I hope you will forgive me for reading this morning, but I hope by reading, I can relate to you what God can do for you in time of sorrow.

We had always known that our little Eddy could not live a normal life span. Of course, none of us have a promise of tomorrow, but with Eddy, the doctors had told us they didn't see how he could live to be twelve years of age. So in the back of our minds, there was the knowledge that we would have to give Eddy up one day. I recall one particular year when Eddy was about seven years old that I decided Eddy was going to die that year. I bought an outfit of clothes to bury him in, put them up to save, and spent one miserable year waiting for Eddy to die. But God was not ready yet, and at the end of the year, I still had my Eddy.

One thing I have learned: God always knows best. When Eddy became a little difficult to handle in church and I became concerned he would disturb the congregation in the large church I was attending, I began to miss a few Sundays. Before too long, I had stopped taking Eddy to church. Suppose God had taken my Eddy then. Don't kid yourself people. Yes, you can worship God at home, but you can stay much nearer to God by going to church and associating with Christian friends. God was so considerate to us to lead us to a small friendly church where I could carry my Eddy and never worry about disturbing those around us. And you know something, I don't recall Eddy becoming disturbed but about a couple of times at Chattahoochee (Baptist Church). Most of the time, he would sleep or else lay his head on our shoulder and look at us so sweetly. You know what I think? I think God had his hand in the matter. He let me get back to church where I belonged, and I *thank* him for it.

God was so kind to us in many ways. In Eddy's death itself, he was so merciful. Eddy was not sick for any length of time. The only indication we had that anything was wrong was the fact that he wasn't eating well, but this happened quite often.

The night he died, he didn't eat supper well, and I lay down with him after supper and went to sleep with him on my shoulder. I awoke about the time Jobo was getting off from work, and because Eddy didn't eat much supper, I fixed some milk and tried to give it to him. But I couldn't get him to take the milk. There was quite a change in my Eddy in the few hours since I went to sleep. I had never been around death before, but down deep in my heart, I knew Eddy was dying. As soon as Jobo came in, we rushed him to the hospital. He died within a very short while after we got there. I thank God for his mercy in Eddy's death. I thank God he didn't let Eddy suffer so before he died.

I am so grateful to God that he let me live to take care of Eddy all his life. I had always worried about what would happen to Eddy if I died first—another evidence of God's mercy in our lives.

Many times I had told Jobo I could not face the time when Eddy would die (and I really didn't think I could), and now the time had come. What could I do? Nothing. Death is inevitable for us all, but with God's help, we can come through this time. About three weeks before Eddy died, I woke up one night and had to get up and write. I wasn't satisfied until I had written about three pages. These three pages turned out to be words of comfort to me. Why did I have to get up and write? God was making the way a little easier for me.

The day of Eddy's death, I took some medicine, which left me feeling drugged all day. The following day, the day of the funeral, I decided to put my trust in God instead of in medicine. What a difference it made! God is so much more powerful. God's mercy was evident again.

Wednesday morning, the day of the funeral, was a beautiful spring day right in the middle of winter. The sun was shining bright, and the birds were singing when we left the house that morning. God knew a lovely day would make it a little easier on me.

I thank God for friends in time of sorrow. I had never realized before just how much friends can mean in times of sorrow—friends who would get out of their bed in the middle of the night to come and offer their consolation, friends who worked around the house to help in any way, friends who sent flowers or came to visit, friends who sent cards or remembered you in any way, friends who furnished food, and friends who attended the funeral. Every little act of kindness means so much.

Jobo, the boys, and I were at the funeral home about an hour before the funeral. I sat down by the casket for my last moments with my Eddy. I took hold of his hand. I felt an inner strength I had not felt before. I felt at peace with God. The time had come to say goodbye to Eddy, and I was going to make it because I had God on my side.

We left the funeral home and started toward the church. Jobo, the boys, and I always sang on our way to church. Little Jimmy made the remark that Eddy wouldn't feel right without us singing so on the way to church, we sang a song just for the little Eddy, and I believe he heard it.

We arrived at the church, and I still had that inner calmness. The church to me looked beautiful. The flowers were arranged so nicely, and there were my friends again. And such sweet music!

I had wondered if it would be a problem selecting the preacher for Eddy's service, but it wasn't. It just seemed the right thing to have Brother Paul. The fact that he married Jobo and I and the fact that he was handicapped in speech and in hearing made him the logical one to handle my Eddy's service. I don't know if anyone else heard the message or not, but I did. And I'll always remember some of the things he said. How some people were more handicapped than my Eddy, how some were handicapped by hate, how some had the ability to speak but could not speak for God, how some could see but could not see God, and how some could walk but could not walk for God. He said Eddy was a silent preacher for God. I had not thought of this before. He was submissive and had not (overtly) sinned against God. I had the assurance that Eddy was with God. How wonderful to know that even though Eddy could not be with me anymore in this world, I could go to meet him at some future date.

"Blessed are they that mourn for they shall be comforted."

Do I believe this? Yes, I know that it is true for I have passed this way, and I have felt the nearness of the comforter.

Yes, there have been times when I have been lonely for the little brown-eyed boy. There have been times when I longed to hold the little one once more. But I can look back to that day when God was near, and because he was near, I can look ahead to the day when I will see my Eddy again. I know I have been saved, and I believe we will meet again. If I ever doubted my salvation, I doubt it no more.

I don't believe I could have had that inner calmness God gave to me unless I had been one of his children. I don't believe I could have said goodbye if I had no hope of seeing him again. I thank God from the bottom of my heart for his comfort in time of sorrow.

Appendix 777

THE PEACE OF GOD

Keeping at Peace in a Troubled World

Philippians 4:1–8

I. THE CONDITION THAT AFFECTS PEACE

1.   UNITY

"I beseech Euodias and beseech Syntyche, that they be of the same mind in the Lord."

—Verse 2

Something is very wonderful about brothers and sisters in the Lord dwelling in unity. It is something that God places a high premium on. We can have unity because of a common bond. We fellowship around Christ based on a common experience: the new birth. When we are facing a storm, the support we receive from our spiritual family is of inestimable worth.

Something had disrupted the unity at Philippi. Two women, Euodias and Syntyche, were at odds with each other. Paul does not specify what the problem was. It is possible it was a minor matter that these women did not see "eye to eye" on. If that were the case, it may not have blown up to major proportions yet. Paul, however, realizing the potential for mischief addresses the situation. He understood that where there is a lack of unity, the overall peace and calm of the church will be affected.

How is unity achieved? Paul instructed them to be of the same mind *in the Lord*. How can two individuals be of the same mind? He had previously taught them in chapter 2:5–11 to **"let this mind be in you, which was also in Christ Jesus."** The following verses laid out in very plain detail what the mind of Christ was and how he humbled himself as a servant.

Only as each Christian seeks the mind of Christ, being conformed to his image, can we be of one mind and spirit. If we seek to be like him, we will strive to put others first and exhibit a true servant's heart. When there is unity, peace can flourish.

2.   HELPING OTHERS TO UNITY

> **"And I intreat thee also, true yokefellow, help those women which laboured with me in the gospel, with Clement also, and with other my fellow labourers, whose names are in the book of life."**

> —Verse 3

Two factors caused Paul to conclude that these women needed help reconciling their differences. First, there was the potential of the division escalating to include the entire church body. Secondly, the very fact that the apostle intervened indicates it was evident to all that these women were past the point of settling it on their own. That Paul knew about the contention also indicates someone had written to him and expressed their concern about it. Since they were unable to come to an agreement on their own, they needed help to guide them to unity.

Paul outlines two reasons why it was necessary to restore unity between the two. They were both Christian sisters who names were in the Book of Life. Not only that, they both had been used greatly of the Lord in the past. Both had been very beneficial to the work of Paul and of Clement also. These were not your average busybodies. They were genuine Christians with genuine love who had developed a genuine disagreement.

To ensure a fertile ground on which peace could prosper, they needed a mediator from the church to guide them to reconciliation. This "yokefellow" was not identified but must have been a prominent person in the church, perhaps the pastor.

In all of this discussion, the problem is never specified, the mediator is never identified, and we know precious little about Clement who is named in this passage. But those matters are of little consequence. What *is* vitally important in this scripture is the fact that there was friction between sisters in the Lord. The Holy Spirit considered unity important enough to include this example in scripture.

Nothing disrupts peace of mind more than disunity, and where there is unity, peace can flourish.

II. ATTITUDES THAT CONTRIBUTE TO PEACE

1. A REJOICING HEART

"Rejoice in the Lord always: and again I say, Rejoice."

—Verse 4

Much of the turmoil we may feel in our hearts is there because we have allowed it to be there. Our emotional well-being is tied very closely to certain preexisting attitudes that determine how we view things. For example, a pessimistic attitude will determine that in every situation, something is bound to go wrong. It then becomes a self-fulfilling prophecy. The expectancy of approaching problems causes the person to actually look for difficulties, and the pessimist *will* find them.

If negative attitudes can contribute to chaos, then the positive outlooks that only a Christian knows can contribute to peace.

A heart that rejoices in the Lord will be a breath of fresh air to any environment. There will be no room in a rejoicing heart for pessimism or any other negative attitude. Wherever this person goes, his presence will bless and uplift all those around him.

This does not mean the person is out of touch with reality or he is living in a fantasy world. He has seen the harsh reality of the world but tempers that view by looking at a loving God and reveling in his goodness.

There is so much for the Christian to rejoice about. He is a child of God. He has a blessed hope to look forward to. One day, the Lord shall appear and take him to his eternal home. There he shall partake in the marriage supper of the Lamb and shall be blessed by a holy love for all eternity. Until that day, there are the blessings of family, home, and a daily walk with the Lord that can sustain him.

How can a Christian who has felt God's touch and experienced his love *not* rejoice?

2. A GENTLE BEHAVIOR

"Let your moderation (gentleness) **be known unto all men. The Lord is at hand."**

—Verse 5 (emphasis added)

The person who is given to extremes will find himself in constant turmoil. He is carried away by his emotions and reacts strongly to any imagined slight. He will constantly demand "his rights."

The person of a gentle demeanor will not be carried to extremes. Sure, he has emotions and is not afraid to express them, but he will not be controlled or consumed by them. His is an *unselfish* attitude. He will behave in a gentle manner toward others and will not be given to strong reactions, which may cause disturbances. This is a behavior that can only be affected by the work of the Holy Spirit in a Christian.

This person walks as Jesus walked. He follows the example of his Lord who sought no reputation for himself.

The motivation that the Apostle Paul gives to walk in this manner is this: the Lord is at hand. This is truly sobering, for the one who will judge our motives knows what it is like to walk in gentleness.

3.   A CALM SPIRIT

> **"Be careful** (anxious) **for nothing."**
>
> —Verse 6a (emphasis added)

What Paul is basically saying to them is "Don't worry!" Worrying about something is absolutely useless. Let's take a look at what worry actually accomplishes.

Worry gets nothing done. Worry comes up with no solution. It is through calm deliberation that most solutions are found, not through worry.

Worry robs you of peace. It causes you to be constantly "on edge."

Worry doesn't take God into consideration. We worry about what we are going to do and forget God is in sovereign control. It takes our focus off Christ.

Worry also affects you physically. It is great for causing ulcers, tension, and hair loss. It can literally make you sick and contribute to heart problems.

The bottom line is *worry is a lack of faith*. Instead of trusting the Lord, we worry. What are *we* going to do?

In the latter part of verse 6, there is a *positive action* that ties in with this command not to worry, but we will cover that just a little later.

4.   A PURE MIND

> **"Finally, brethren, whatsoever things are true, whatsoever things are honest, whatsoever**

things are just, whatsoever things are pure, whatsoever things are lovely, whatsoever things are of good report; if there by any virtue, and if there be any praise, think on these things."

—Verse 8

Nothing will clutter a mind more than garbage. What occupies our minds will determine our actions. This verse teaches us to clear our minds of useless baggage and fill it with something more constructive.

One thing we need to remove is a negative attitude. Why must people always be willing to think the worse about another? Why must we always say something can't be done? Remove that pessimistic attitude from your thoughts.

We need to battle any impure thoughts. We must banish any tendency to dishonesty or baseness.

But it is not that easy to fight the battle for the mind. We must do more than just say "I'm not going to think on those things." We must fill our minds with pure things so there is no room for the impure.

Fill your mind with God's word, and sin will not find an easy resting place there. Always carry a positive attitude (things of good report) and negativism will not drag you down. Dwell on holiness, and you will not be subject to dishonesty.

As your mind dwells on pure things, you will find a peace of mind that is not possible with a cluttered mind.

III. THE ACTION THAT BRINGS PEACE

1. DON'T WORRY, PRAY!

"Be careful for nothing; but in everything by prayer and supplication with thanksgiving let your requests be made known unto God."

—Verse 6

There is a positive step you can take that will produce peace in your life. After dealing with unity, which affects peace and the attitude that contributes to peace, Paul specifies the action that actually yields to peace.

When faced with difficulties, *don't worry, pray!* Once again, in scripture, prayer is designated as the key to peace of mind. Instead of wrestling with a problem while trying to find a solution, take it to God. Lay it at his feet. Let him figure it all out and then submit to his direction.

The very next verse clearly states that when you go to God in prayer, there is a *specific result*.

2. THE RESULT OF PRAYING

"And the peace of God, which passeth all understanding, shall keep your hearts and mind through Christ Jesus."

—Verse 7

The direct result of praying is the peace of God permeates your entire being, heart, and mind.

This peace is beyond understanding and, therefore, defies description. It is a supernatural peace, infiltrating the furthest recesses of your soul.

The source of this peace is God himself. It is his peace, the peace *of* God. When God's child falls to his knees in prayer, an overwhelming calm sent from the throne of Heaven penetrates his soul. It is while on his knees that he is obedient to the command to "pray without ceasing." It is while bowing before the king that the Christian demonstrates his submission.

I want you to notice what this verse says about the peace of God. You don't have to worry about keeping the peace of God. IT WILL KEEP YOU! When we pray to the Father in the name of Jesus and submit ourselves to his will, his peace keeps us in a state of calm assurance. It is indicative of the confidence we have in him that he hears our prayer and cares deeply for his own.

May God's peace keep you in Christ Jesus.

About the Author

Jimmy Foster is an ordained Baptist minister with over forty years in the ministry. He has served several churches as pastor, interim pastor, or associate pastor. his experience in the business world gives him a unique insight into the everyday struggles of the average person.

He makes his home in the north Georgia mountains—God's beautiful creation.

CPSIA information can be obtained
at www.ICGtesting.com
Printed in the USA
LVOW08s0103210517
535252LV00001B/14/P